Frank Berger

Creating Competitive Advantage with Electroni

A Study of the German Insurance Industry

Frank Berger

Creating Competitive Advantage with Electronic Commerce

A Study of the German Insurance Industry

diplom.de

Bibliografische Information der Deutschen Nationalbibliothek:

Bibliografische Information der Deutschen Nationalbibliothek: Die Deutsche Bibliothek verzeichnet diese Publikation in der Deutschen Nationalbibliografie; detaillierte bibliografische Daten sind im Internet über http://dnb.d-nb.de/ abrufbar.

Copyright © 1999 Diplomica Verlag GmbH
Druck und Bindung: Books on Demand GmbH, Norderstedt Germany
ISBN: 978-3-8386-2358-0

http://www.diplom.de/e-book/218172/creating-competitive-advantage-with-electronic-commerce

Frank Berger

Creating Competitive Advantage with Electronic Commerce
A Study of the German Insurance Industry

MBA
am Hemley Management College
Fachbereich Business Administration
Dezember 1999 Abgabe

***Diplomarbeiten* Agentur**
Dipl. Kfm. Dipl. Hdl. Björn Bedey
Dipl. Wi.-Ing. Martin Haschke
und Guido Meyer GbR

Hermannstal 119 k
22119 Hamburg

agentur@diplom.de
www.diplom.de

ID 2358
Berger, Frank: Creating Competitive Advantage with Electronic Commerce: A Study of the German Insurance Industry / Frank Berger · Hamburg: Diplomarbeiten Agentur, 2000
Zugl.: Hemley Management College, MBA, 1999

Dipl. Kfm. Dipl. Hdl. Björn Bedey, Dipl. Wi.-Ing. Martin Haschke & Guido Meyer GbR
Diplomarbeiten Agentur, http://www.diplom.de, Hamburg 2000
Printed in Germany

Diplomarbeiten Agentur

Wissensquellen gewinnbringend nutzen

Qualität, Praxisrelevanz und Aktualität zeichnen unsere Studien aus. Wir bieten Ihnen im Auftrag unserer Autorinnen und Autoren Wirtschaftsstudien und wissenschaftliche Abschlussarbeiten – Dissertationen, Diplomarbeiten, Magisterarbeiten, Staatsexamensarbeiten und Studienarbeiten zum Kauf. Sie wurden an deutschen Universitäten, Fachhochschulen, Akademien oder vergleichbaren Institutionen der Europäischen Union geschrieben. Der Notendurchschnitt liegt bei 1,5.

Wettbewerbsvorteile verschaffen – Vergleichen Sie den Preis unserer Studien mit den Honoraren externer Berater. Um dieses Wissen selbst zusammenzutragen, müssten Sie viel Zeit und Geld aufbringen.

http://www.diplom.de bietet Ihnen unser vollständiges Lieferprogramm mit mehreren tausend Studien im Internet. Neben dem Online-Katalog und der Online-Suchmaschine für Ihre Recherche steht Ihnen auch eine Online-Bestellfunktion zur Verfügung. Inhaltliche Zusammenfassungen und Inhaltsverzeichnisse zu jeder Studie sind im Internet einsehbar.

Individueller Service – Gerne senden wir Ihnen auch unseren Papierkatalog zu. Bitte fordern Sie Ihr individuelles Exemplar bei uns an. Für Fragen, Anregungen und individuelle Anfragen stehen wir Ihnen gerne zur Verfügung. Wir freuen uns auf eine gute Zusammenarbeit

Ihr Team der *Diplomarbeiten* Agentur

Dipl. Kfm. Dipl. Hdl. Björn Bedey –
Dipl. Wi.-Ing. Martin Haschke ――
und Guido Meyer GbR ―――――

Hermannstal 119 k ―――――
22119 Hamburg ―――――

Fon: 040 / 655 99 20 ―――――
Fax: 040 / 655 99 222 ―――――

agentur@diplom.de ―――――
www.diplom.de ―――――

For my wife Elke who gave me support all the time during my studies and Patrick F. who often missed his father in the last three years.

Acknowledgments

In the course of this dissertation a fieldwork was carried out. The author wants to say thanks to all persons who took part at the questionaire research and made it possible for me to get sound data as basis for this piece of work.

Special thanks to the CIO's who invited me for an interview. It was very helpful for me discussing strategic as well as operational issues on the subject of electronic commerce within the German insurance industry.

CONTENTS

ABSTRACT 1

1   INTRODUCTION 2

    1.1   OBJECTIVES 2
    1.2   APPROACH..3

2   HYPOTHESIS AND OBJECTIVES 4

3   THE GERMAN INSURANCE INDUSTRY 5

    3.1   STATUS QUO 5
    3.2   FUTURE TRENDS 7

4   LITERATURE REVIEW 10

    4.1   E-COMMERCE - CHARACTERISTICS AND PERSPECTIVES 10
    4.2   INSURANCE PRODUCTS AND SERVICES IN ELECTRONIC COMMERCE 14
    4.3   ELECTRONIC COMMERCE AND THE VALUE CHAIN 17
    4.4   COMPETITIVE ADVANTAGE 20
    4.5   BUSINESS PROCESSES WITHIN THE INSURANCE INDUSTRY 26
    4.6   ORGANISATIONAL IMPLICATIONS FOR ELECTRONIC COMMERCE....................................31
    4.7   SUCCESS FACTORS FOR ELECTRONIC COMMERCE 34
    4.8   SUMMARY OF LITERATURE RESEARCH 35

5   FIELDWORK...39

    5.1   RESEARCH AND OBJECTIVES 39
    5.2   METHODOLOGY AND SCOPE - OUTLINE 39
    5.3   QUESTIONNAIRE ON E-COMMERCE...40
    5.4   INTERVIEWS WITH CIO'S...41
    5.5   LIMITATIONS OF THE RESEARCH...41

6   FINDINGS AND ANALYSIS OF FIELDWORK DATA 42

    6.1   GENERAL FINDINGS..42
    6.2   FUTURE INDUSTRY TRENDS..44
    6.3   CONSUMER PROFILES, EXPECTATIONS AND BEHAVIOUR 47
    6.4   PRODUCTS AND SERVICES..50
    6.5   VALUE CHAIN AND COMPETITIVE ADVANTAGE...53
    6.6   BUSINESS PROCESSES...59
    6.7   FOCUSED AREAS 63
    6.8   CONSTRAINTS 64
    6.9   SUMMARY OF FIELDWORK 66

7   CONCLUSIONS...67

    7.1   CONCLUSIONS DRAWN FROM THE LITERATURE 67
    7.2   CONCLUSIONS DRAWN FROM THE FIELDWORK 68
    7.3   FINAL CONCLUSIONS-CORRELATIONS BETWEEN THE LITERATURE AND FIELDWORK 69

8   RECOMMENDATIONS 70

9   APPENDICES...73

    9.1   APPENDIX 1: 73
    9.2   APPENDIX 2: 74
    9.3   APPENDIX 3: QUESTIONNAIRE 75
    9.4   APPENDIX 4: INTERVIEW GUIDE 80
    9.5   APPENDIX 5: 83

10   BIBLIOGRAPHY...84

Abbreviations

ANX	Automotive Network eXchange
BCG	The Boston Consulting Group
B2B	Business-to-business
B2C	Business-to-consumer
CEO	Chief executive officer
CIO	Chief information officer
CRM	Customer relationship management
CSF	Critical success factor
DM	Deutsche Mark
EC	Electronic commerce
ERP	Enterprise resource planning
e.g.	exempli gratia
i.e.	id est
HR	Human resources
KSF	Key success factors
MBA	Master of Business Administration
P&C	Property and casualty
PEST	Political, economic, social, technical
POS	Point of Sales /Point of Service
PVC	Physical value chain
PWC	Price WaterhouseCoopers
R & D	Research and development
SFA	Salesforce automation
TV	Television
VVC	Virtual value chain
www	World Wide Web

Figures

FIGURE 1: PEST-ANALYSIS...5
FIGURE 2: PORTER'S 5 FORCES 7
FIGURE 3: LIFE CYCLE-MODEL..8
FIGURE 4: CRITICAL SUCCESS FACTORS..9
FIGURE 5: AREAS OF ELECTRONIC COMMERCE..11
FIGURE 6: ELECTRONIC COMMERCE IN INDUSTRIAL VIEW (BERRYMAN/HARRINGTON/LAYTON-RODIN/REROLLE (1998)13
FIGURE 7: PRODUCTS SUITABLE FOR ELECTRONIC COMMERCE (SCHINZER 1997, P.24)..........................14
FIGURE 8: CLASSICAL VALUE CHAIN (PORTER 1985, P. 37)..17
FIGURE 9: REAL-VIRTUAL VALUE CHAIN (WEIBER/KOLLMANN 1999, P. 50)..18
FIGURE 10: NETWORKING OF BUSINESS PARTNERS; (SAUTER 1999, P. 109) 19
FIGURE 11: COMPETITIVE ADVANTAGE (GRANT 1995; P. 121) 20
FIGURE 12: PORTER'S GENERIC STRATEGIES...21
FIGURE 13: SUCCESS FACTORS (WEIBER/ KOLLMANN 1999, P. 59) 22
FIGURE 14: RETHINKING THE CLASSICAL ORGANISATION (FOLLOWING HAGEL/SINGER 1999; P. 62).......23
FIGURE 15: ELECTRONIC COMMERCE BENEFITS (SAUTER 1999, P. 103)...24
FIGURE 16: PLAYERS WITHIN THE INSURANCE INDUSTRY 26
FIGURE 17: DIFFERENCES BETWEEN B2B AND B2C ELECTRONIC COMMERCE......................................27
FIGURE 18: B2B-STRATEGIES 27
FIGURE 19: B2B PROCESSES WITHIN THE GERMAN INSURANCE INDUSTRY 28
FIGURE 20: THE MCKINSEY 7 S- MODEL (PETERS/WATERMAN 1982, P. 32)..31
FIGURE 21: SUMMARY TABLE OF AUTHORS AND THEIR KEYFINDINGS...38
FIGURE 22: PROFESSIONAL BACKGROUND OF RESPONDENTS 42
FIGURE 23: COMPOSITION OF PROJECT TEAMS 43
FIGURE 24: SALES CHANNELS WITHIN THE GERMAN INSURANCE INDUSTRY 43
FIGURE 25: CHANGE IN SALES CHANNELS 46
FIGURE 26: SOCIO-DEMOCRATIC TRENDS 47
FIGURE 27: EVALUATION OF ONLINE-SHOPPING...48
FIGURE 28: PREFERRED PRODUCTS FOR ONLINE SHOPPING 48
FIGURE 29: PRODUCTS/SERVICES FROM CUSTOMERS' POINT OF VIEW...49
FIGURE 30: SUITABILITY OF INSURANCE PRODUCTS...50
FIGURE 31: SERVICE OFFERINGS 52
FIGURE 32: FOCUS ON CORE COMPETENCIES 53
FIGURE 33: MAIN BENEFITS OF ELECTRONIC COMMERCE 54
FIGURE 34: DIAGRAM STRATEGIC IMPACT 56
FIGURE 35: SOURCES OF COMPETITIVE ADVANTAGE..57
FIGURE 36: LINKING OF STATEMENTS TO ELECTRONIC COMMERCE BENEFITS.......................................57
FIGURE 37: AREAS FOR COMPETITIVE ADVANTAGE- RESEARCH RESULT 58
FIGURE 38: EVALUATION OF B2C PROCESSES 59
FIGURE 39: BUSINESS PROCESSES IN THE BUSINESS-TO-BUSINESS FIELD 60
FIGURE 40: INFORMATION MANAGEMENT...62
FIGURE 41: AREAS IN FOCUS...63
FIGURE 42: CONSTRAINTS FOR ELECTRONIC COMMERCE 64
FIGURE 43: FRAMEWORK OF IMPLEMENTATION OF EC PRINCIPLES 70

Abstract

Electronic commerce is a dynamically evolving method of doing business in almost every industry and is changing the way companies do business. As electronic commerce is quickly increasing within some industries such as computers, software and retail banking the question arises whether and how insurance companies can profit too. This dissertation evaluates the impact of electronic commerce on the German insurance industry with the overall goal of creating competitive advantage.

The hypothesis addressed in this dissertation is: "Electronic commerce provides an excellent means for insurance companies for creating competitive advantage."

The dissertation proceeds by reviewing the literature for definitions and perspectives of electronic commerce, the suitability of electronic commerce for insurance products and services, the impact on existing business processes and value chains as well as the sources for creating competitive advantage within a mature insurance industry. Additionally, its organizational implications have also been examined.

This dissertation contains fieldwork on the issues focused on in theory. Primary data was gathered using a questionnaire and a few interviews that were conducted with Chief Information Officers. The results of these activities were analysed and discussed by comparing them with both theory and experiences of other industries.

The study revealed that German insurance companies have discovered the internet medium and with it electronic commerce in order to create competitive advantage by reengineering their current business processes as well as providing premium customer service. Furthermore, it was found that standardized private customer business is expected to move online within the next 10 years. The study also determined that the persons questioned do not expect that traditional value chains will be dramatically affected as is often predicted in the literature on the subject or as has already happened in other industries.

The conclusion is that electronic commerce is an excellent medium for (German) insurance companies to create competitive advantage in many areas. All classical generic strategies it can be supported by electronic commerce even if the differentation focus (service/quality) is probably the most successful owing to the industry lifecycle of the German insurance industry. The greatest winners will be the first movers.

1   Introduction

1.1 *Objectives*

The aim of this dissertation is to investigate and evaluate the complex subject of electronic commerce according to its strategic impact and suitability for the German insurance industry in order to create competitive advantage. In more detail, the author wants to find out in which areas electronic commerce is able to create competitive advantage and how electronic commerce is best implemented. This shall be done by analysing the literature and taking experiences and examples from other industries. Additionally, the author wants to investigate how German insurance companies think about this subject, what kind of actions they have already undertaken or have planned.

A personal note:

I have chosen this subject because I work as a presales IT consultant for insurance companies with "debis Systemhaus", a subsidiary of the Daimler-Chrysler group. My learning objectives with this dissertation are to become more familiar with the subject of electronic commerce on both the technical and the business side. This dissertation should help me to increase my knowledge of electronic commerce, especially the opportunities it provides for the insurance industry and the problems management is faced with during its implementation. In order to maximise the benefits of my MBA study I have chosen an area which covers my personal interests and is as well a major management issue amongst German insurance companies. It is my intention to get a foothold within the electronic commerce consulting business.

1.2 Approach

In the first section of this work the hypothesis and objectives are briefly defined. The second section deals with current management literature and what is written and said about electronic commerce in general. Theory shall be compared to practice by examining the experience other industries have had with electronic commerce. Additionally, the employment and specific characteristics of electronic commerce with reference to the insurance industry shall be outlined and discussed. It is the intention of the author to work out the areas that enable insurance companies to create competitive advantage within industry specifics.

In the third section the fieldwork that has been carried out by the author is dealt with , i.e. the scope, methodology as well as the limitations of the questionnaire and the interviews are briefly explained.

The research findings shall be the subject of discussion in the fourth section. Comparisons to the statements of literature as well as findings of some secondary data sources shall help to identify any difference between theory and practice.

In section five, conclusions shall be drawn from both the literature on the subject and the fieldwork that was carried out as to whether and how insurance companies can create competitive advantage using EC or not. Furthermore, the author wants to identify the correlations between theory and practice.

The dissertation will close with recommendations for successfully implementing electronic commerce on the basis of the results that have been worked out by the author in the course of this work.

2 Hypothesis and Objectives

The hypothesis underlying this dissertation is that

"Electronic commerce provides an excellent means for insurance companies to create competitive advantage."

The author understands the expression "excellent " in this connection as extremely well suited in order to match industry specifics as well as future trends and market demands. With this dissertation I want to investigate the impact of the internet on the German insurance industry and the opportunities that ensue from it in order to create competitive advantage within a mature insurance industry. In more detail, the author is interested in the areas that enable insurance companies to create sustained competitive advantage over competitors by deploying electronic commerce as well as the strategies that are most likely to be successful for implementation.

- The status quo and the main trends for the future within the German insurance industry
- The characteristics of and the perspectives for electronic commerce
- The suitability of the insurance product and the services that can be combined with it
- The role and necessity of electronic commerce with reference to the reengineering of business processes within the German insurance industry
- The impact of electronic commerce on the value chain and the industry structure
- The possibility of creating competitive advantage by deploying electronic commerce within the insurance industry
- Suitable processes that can be depicted with electronic commerce
- Implications of electronic commerce for organisational issues
- Limitations of electronic commerce within the insurance industry

3   The German insurance industry

In order to investigate the suitability of EC for the German insurance industry a brief
look at the macro- and micro environment shall help to determine both the current
situation as well as the main future trends. That way the main criteria for success (key
success factors) of this industry- which form the basis for the creation of competitive
advantage- can be determined.

3.1   Status quo

The macro- and the micro environment have a major impact on industry structure. The
competition also determine the key success factors within an industry. Therefore a PEST
-analysis and the Porter 5-forces framework[1] shall be applied in this section in order to
determine the main trends for the future and the KSF's that are connected with it.

Status quo

A PEST analysis has proven to be very helpful for analysing the macro-environment.

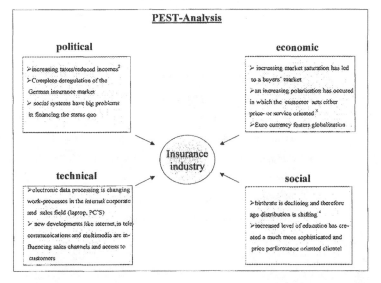

FIGURE 1: PEST-ANALYSIS

---

[1] Porter (1985),p. 5
2 Statistical Yearbook (1998), p.
3 Muth (1982), p. 13
4 Brinkmann (1991), p. 8

With reference to the micro-environment, the Porter 5 forces framework has proven to be an excellent means of determining industry attractiveness and, by implication, the level of competition.

(1) The threat of new entrants into new business:

- The total number of competitors has increased. (direct insurers; special insurers).[1] INEAS, the first internet insurance company operating European-wide has been founded.[2]
- Other industries, especially banks and car-dealers want to satisfy their customers' needs by the idea of "one-stop-shopping", have discovered the insurance "product" and its service-enhancing aspect.[3]

(2) The bargaining power of buyers:

- As a result of steadily growing competition and a price war, customers are becoming more and more powerful.
- Consumer protection organisations and the internet are strengthening the consumers' position through their ratings and price comparisons of different products.

(3) Rivalry between existing competitors:

- The growth rates of premium income in this industry have declined from 9% in 1990 to 2.0 % in 1998, whereby the property and casualty lines (P & C) are declining and the personal insurance lines (health and life) are increasing.[4]
- Competition is forcing mergers and related concentration into insurance groups in order to realise "economies of scale"; the total number of German insurance companies has continually decreased in the last years[5] and will be cut in half by 2010.[6] (10 greatest companies cover 40% of market share)

---

[1] Statistical Yearbook (1998), p. 36
[2] http://www.ineas.com
[3] Muth (1994), p. 294
[4] Appendix 1, p. 62
[5] Statistical Yearbook (1998), p. 38
[6] Mummert & Partner (1999) http://www.mummert.de/deutsch/press/ppbz0209.html

(4) The bargaining power of suppliers:

- Suppliers do not exist in this industry since the companies do not need any raw materials, parts or even finished products.

(5) The threat of substitute products:

- In property and casualty insurance no real substitutes exist. The only kind of substitute is self insurance, i.e. people insure only parts or none of their risks.
- In the provision for old age and in the field of fixed interest, investments like real estate, stocks, bonds, investment funds and other financial products of greater importance are becoming substitute products.[1]

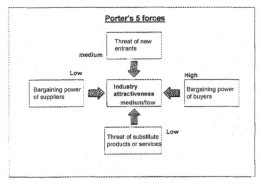

FIGURE 2: PORTER'S 5 FORCES

3.2   Future trends

According to the analysis of the macro- and micro-environment in the preceding paragraph, four main areas of change can be determined.[2]

Main trends

o   *Industry structure:*

Mergers are influencing industry structure; "economies of scale" require greater insurance companies. Additionally, banks are moving into the insurance business more and more.

---

[1] Statistical Yearbook (1998), pp. 33
[2] Feilmeier (1998), p 59

7

o   *Customers*

Customers are becoming more sophisticated and powerful. Price and
performance are becoming the main areas of competition. (Customisation?)

o   *Products*

Owing to deregulation, customers and competition are forcing insurance
companies to greater product flexibility with effects on the life cycle as well as
time-to-market and contract/product administration.

o   *Technology*

Technological change, especially the internet and telecommunications are going
to influence the business processes and sales channels within the insurance
industry[1].

Based on the lifecycle concept, the insurance industry could be labelled as mature.
This concept, originally coming from marketing in order to explain the behaviour of
products within a specific market[2] can also be applied to an industry. It provides very
helpful information about demand, cash-flow and growth within an industry.

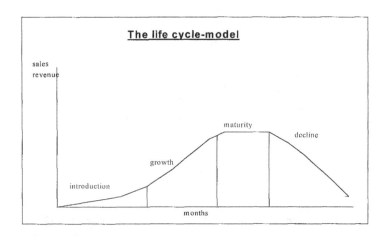

FIGURE 3: LIFE CYCLE-MODEL

---

[1] Mummert & Partner (1999), http://www.mummert.de/deutsch/press/990509.html
[2] Kotler (1995), p. 355

The stage of evolution plays a major role when determining the key success factors within an industry. According to Grant, growth or decline in demand and changes of technology over a product life cycle have an impact on industry structure and competition and thus the sources of competitive advantage (key success factors KSF)[1]. With reference to mature industries these are generally:

- Cost-efficiency scale
- Process innovation
- Buyer selection

In more detail the CSF for the insurance industry depend on the customer groups but nevertheless confirm this statement.

Private sector	Commercial sector	Industrial sector
* price-performance ratio * advice and aid services * standardised and customised products	* quality of advice * advice about risk assessment / loss prevention * customised global coverage	* high underwriting capacity * customised coverage * global international programmes * knowledge about different industries and their specific needs * financial power

FIGURE 4: CRITICAL SUCCESS FACTORS

[1] Grant (1995), p. 236

4   Literature review

4.1   E-Commerce - characteristics and perspectives

The term E-Commerce has its origin from the study „ Management in the 90s",
undertaken by the MIT. According to this study the main idea behind E-Commerce is
that communication between organisations is becoming more important than
communication inside an organisation.[1] Even today there is no standardised definition of
electronic commerce and owing to the manifold utilizability of Electronic commerce
this is very difficult to do.

In general it can be said that the understanding of electronic commerce has changed
from the technical handling of business processes to a separate "market" which implies
that commerce has become the focus of attention.[2] A lot of people regard electronic
commerce very specifically as "buying and selling products over the internet"[3] which
implies the focus is on the sales- and procurement processes.

On the other hand there is a more general definition from Schinzer and Thome which
states that "E-Commerce enables the completely digital settling of business processes
between companies (themselves) and their customers over global public and private
networks (internet)."[4] This implies that electronic commerce is not only about buying
and selling but also information interchange as well as the integration of various and
general value chains and business processes.[5]

The differentiation of electronic commerce from the term "e-business" is not that clear.
Langmarck and Baumann/Kistner regard electronic commerce as part of e-business
which focuses on the external marketing and sales processes of a corporation whereas e-
business implies internal processes additionally and thus the general implication of
internet technologies .[6] However, the author finds the artificial distinction of expressions
such as e-business and e-commerce as hair splitting since the general view of electronic

---

[1] Magnus (1997), p.32 ff
[2] Koch/Wagner (1998), p. 1643
[3] Bliemel/Fassot/Theobald (1999), p. 2
[4] Schinzer/Thomae (1997), p. 1
[5] Hermanns/Sauter (1999), p. 15
[6] Baumann/Kistner (1999),pp. 302; Langmarck (1999),pp. 10

commerce and e-business in the end are the same things. The author is of the opinion that if electronic commerce is to be successful it cannot end at a company's portal. The author views electronic commerce from the general point of view, e.g. the digital handling of business processes.

Hermanns and Sauter distinguish between three types of possible supplier and buyer which the following figure shows.[1]

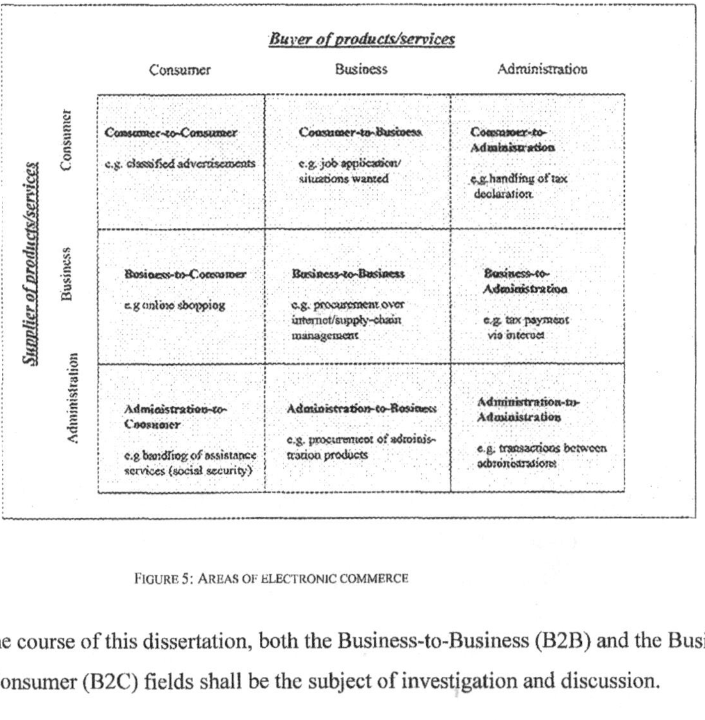

FIGURE 5: AREAS OF ELECTRONIC COMMERCE

In the course of this dissertation, both the Business-to-Business (B2B) and the Business-to-Consumer (B2C) fields shall be the subject of investigation and discussion.

---

[1] Hermanns/Sauter (1999), p. 23

The principle of electronic commerce

Bliemel/ Fassot/ Theobald explain electronic commerce as the combination of different technical principles. These are database systems for storing and selective retrieval of information, communication networks for data interchange between the several IT systems as well as multimedia, i.e. the integrative usage of dynamic media such as video or audio and static media such as texts and graphics. Further characteristics of electronic commerce are the hypertext principle which stands for the non-linear connection of information through links and the interactive possibilities associated with it, i.e. the user has the opportunity to change contents and trigger off transactions.[1]

Growth of online users

However, owing to the different definitions and views of electronic commerce a lot of different growth predictions exist - and therefore different estimations on turnover development exist.[2] The worldwide growth of online population, so predicts International Data Corporation, will grow from 140 mil in 1998 up to 500 mil. in 2003 wherby the German and the Asian region will catch up with the U.S.[3]

With reference to the German market, gfk -a German research company- found that the number of online-users in Germany increased by 40 % between June '98 and February '99 up to 8.4 mil. users.[4] Similar results were found by another study from Jupiter Research which even predicts that Germany will be the leading European E-Commerce market in the future. By 2002, Germany's online population will amount to 27.4 million users, with 40% buying goods off the Internet.[5]

In order to evaluate electronic commerce strategies and the possibilities of creating competitive advantage it is essential to know the profile of its users as well as their habits when using the Internet. However, recent findings made by gfk are that online shopping has increased tremendously - within the last months 2.2 million people have ordered or bought a product online.

---

[1] Bliemel/Fassot/Theobald (1999), pp. 3
[2] Clement/Peters (1998), p. 49
[3] Appendix 2, p. 63
[4] http://194.175.173.244/gfk/presse.php3? 8.6.99
[5] See Dianne, http://www.thestandard.net/articles/article_display/0,1449,1256,00.html (29.7.99)

Development of an electronic insurance market

A study from McKinsey indicates that "the speed with which an electronic marketplace develops for any product will depend on two factors: the inefficiency of current transactions and the sophistication of buyers."[1] Buyer sophistication is defined by Berryman/Harrington/Layton-Rodin/Rerolle as the ability to understand differences between products and to define clear product specifications. Transaction inefficiencies are seen as coming from poor information flow or complex and multi-tier distribution channels. According to these parameters financial services – to which insurance is counted – are a potential candidate for the 2nd electronic commerce wave.

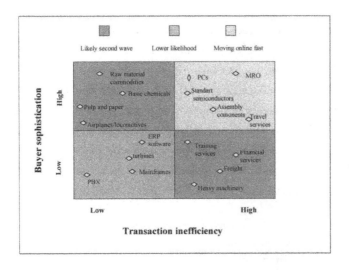

FIGURE 6: ELECTRONIC COMMERCE IN INDUSTRIAL VIEW (BERRYMAN/HARRINGTON/LAYTON-RODIN/REROLLE (1998)

---

[1] Berryman/Harrington/Layton-Rodin/Rerolle (1998), pp. 152-159

4.2   Insurance products and services in electronic commerce

Products

As with every distribution channel so with the positioning of products and services via Internet: product specifics have to be taken into account.[1]

It seems as if the "old" view of insurance - that the need and demand for the insurance product, owing to its specific characteristics (invisible, in need of explanation, connected with negative events), has to be awakened and therefore sold by intermediaries,[2] - has changed in recent years.

Schinzer differentiates products suitable for electronic commerce with regard to price and degree of digitalisation.[3] He states that both digitisable and non digitisable products can be sold over the Internet. The difference between them is only the availability for the customer and the value added potential for the manufacturer owing to the cancellation of logistic costs and intermediaries. In general it can be said that in both categories the low and medium price segment are more suitable for electronic commerce. It is especially the medium price segment of digitisable products to which insurance can be assigned . Schinzer is therefore of the opinion that accident, liability and car insurance are extremely suitable for the internet sales channel.[4]

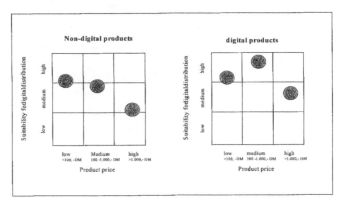

FIGURE 7: PRODUCTS SUITABLE FOR ELECTRONIC COMMERCE (SCHINZER 1997, P.24)

---

[1] Kotler (1994), p. 532
[2] Kühlmann/Kurtenbach/Käßler-Pawelka, (1995) p. 17-18
[3] Schinzer (1997), p.21
[4] Schinzer (1997), p.24

A similar statement comes from Schreiber who states that products that can be delivered electronically are best suited for online-sale, hence insurance would be best suited for electronic commerce. However, with reference to the price, Schwarz/ Freese/ Jaques found that price doesn't really present a hurdle for online insurance since best practice examples have shown annual premium income between 900 and 1,500 DM.[1]

Owing to the complexity and the price of insurance products, most authors are in agreement that standardised private customer products – those that can be counted as commodities - are suitable for electronic commerce.[2] These are liability, car insurance, life term insurance and insurance for homeowners. Hermanns and Sauter even think that life insurance and mortgages can be sold over the net.[3]

Services
The basic responsibility of services is to promote and support the distribution of core products or services that a company offers its customers.[4] The service features a company offers its customers normally revolve around additional benefits in addition to its contractual duties. In the insurance literature typical additional services range from 24-hour help service to loss-prevention information to risk-management advice.[5] The following are mentioned in the literature as typical online-services[6]:

> - Online product information and advice
> - Hotlines for trouble-shooting (FAQ, Guidelines etc.)
> - E-mail enquiries
> - Chatting/discussion groups
> - E-mail complaint management
> - Checking account balances
> - Online order-tracking
> - Track status of claim[7]

---

[1] Schwarz/ Freese/ Jacques (1999), p. 1498-1504
[2] Margheiro/Henry/Cooke/Montes (1998), p. .31-34
[3] Hermanns/Sauter (1999), p. 25
[4] Hünerberg/Mann(1999), p. 282
[5] Kühlmann/Kurtenbach/Käßler-Pawelka (1995), pp. 201-204
[6] Hünerberg/Mann (1999) pp. 282
[7] Margheiro/Henry/Cooke/Montes (1998), p. A4-44

Services offered online are said to be one of the most challenging and lucrative areas of electronic commerce.[1]

As the business world (in mature markets) becomes more customer-centred, customer relationship management (CRM) becomes an important issue. Since the web enables service on a 24/7 basis (24 hours a day/ 7 days a week) it provides greater convenience to the customer than other service channels owing to its independence of opening hours.[2] Offering customer services via the web will therefore be a main trend in the future business world.

Another key trend and characteristic of a mature market is that as goods become standardised (commodities) the scope for differentiation decreases[3]. The combination of growing sophistication and a trend for individualism[4] means that customers require more individual treatment - i.e. products that are customised and individually designed . Classical competitive parameters such as differentiation and cost-leadership are not sufficient in order to make products and services somewhat unique. According to Peppers and Rogers the pardigm of mass production will be replaced by the paradigm of a one-to-one customer relationship which means that products and services will be tailored to the customers' taste and preferences.[5] The new idea on the forefront of this development is that the customer has to be accompanied through the whole buying cycle – which means, in short, establishing a long term customer relationship. [6]

Internet technology and with it electronic commerce provides an excellent means to collect customer data for creating customer profiles in order to offer pre-configured products in which the customer may be interested. Make-to-order products or assemble-to-order products such as in the computer industry (Dell) or in the clothing industry, e.g. Levis, are examples of this big emerging trend. PWC believes that electronic commerce or e-business is all about Customer-Relationship-Management (CRM) and this means personalisation.[7]

---

[1] E-Business Technology Forecast (1999), p. 23
[2] E-Business Technology Forecast (1999), pp. 23-25
[3] Grant (1995),p. 298
[4] Kotler (1994), p.266
[5] Peppers /Rogers (1994), pp. 4-5
[6] Muther (1999), p. 11
[7] E-Business Technology Forecast (1999), p. 46

4.3   Electronic commerce and the value chain

Porter's value chain concept divides a company into important strategic activities or functions which consist of primary and supporting value creating activities. It can be used to analyse sources of competitive advantage either for cost or differentiation (quality).[1] In the figure below the "classical" value chain of an insurance company is shown.

Support activities	Infrastructure, administration & management	Finance, company infrastructure (communication)				
	Human resources	Job offerings, recruitment, staff development, training				
	R & D	Development of new products				
	Procurement	Ordering of office material.				
		No raw materials used	Contract management, customisation, standardisation time to market claim settlement	Claim settlement, specialists.	Marketing, market research sales organisation,	call center Help line Additional service offerings
		Inbound logistics	Operations	Outbound logistics	Marketing/Sales	Service
		Primary activities				

FIGURE 8: CLASSICAL VALUE CHAIN (PORTER 1985, P. 37)

On the whole, the author found two main developments that are connected with Electronic commerce and that will have a strong influence on traditional value chains in almost every industry.[2]

Owing to decreasing interaction costs (internet), there will be an emerging concentration of business activity into specific parts/processes (core competencies) of a value chain within competitive markets .[3] As a result, two main developments will occur:

1. Destruction of existing value chains and thus industries.[4]
2. Creation of virtual value chains[5]

According to Rayport/Sviokla any business today consists of a physical world of resources and a virtual world of information and managers that have to pay attention as to how their companies create value in both worlds. In order to create value in the

---

[1] Porter (1985), pp. 33-47
[2] Evans/Wurzer (1997), p. 19
[3] Hagel/Singer (1999), p. 62
[4] Evans/Wurster (1997), pp.19
[5] Rayport/Sviokla (1995), p. 35

virtual world (Value chain) five activities have to be carried out: *gathering, organising, selecting, synthesising and distributing information.*[1] Transforming the real value chain into a virtual-real value chain means that new and precious information can be drawn on in order to create new value for the marketspace or help to improve the efficiency/quality of real value chains.[2]

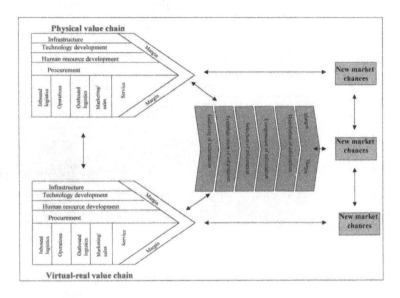

FIGURE 9: REAL-VIRTUAL VALUE CHAIN (WEIBER/KOLLMANN 1999, P. 50)

A good example of this process is USAA, an American insurance company. USAA gathered a lot of data along the whole value chain and started to exploit this data by preparing customer profiles on an individual as well as on an aggregate basis. So USAA designed new products and services to specific customers needs. Today USAA not only provides special coverage for boat owners but also offers financing packages for purchasing boats. By aggregating demand statistics and likely loss ratios it operates now as a smart merchandiser for replacing stolen items for its customers. USAA today is one of the largest direct merchandisers shipping real goods along its PVC on the basis of extracting its VVC. Additionally, it provides shopping services for stolen items.[3]

---

[1] Rayport/Sviokla (1995), pp. 35
[2] Weiber/Kollmann (1999), pp. 49
[3] Rayport/Sviokla (1995), p. 44

Destruction of old value chains is likely to occur because of cheaper information and communication costs which in turn create reengineering possibilities along the value chain between different companies.[1]

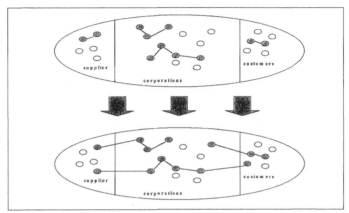

FIGURE 10: NETWORKING OF BUSINESS PARTNERS; (SAUTER 1999, P. 109)

First signs of this development can already be seen in retail banking where customers can now access information and perform transactions. Bank 24 (Deutsche Bank)[2], Advance Bank (Dresdner Bank)[3] are examples of this trend.

Furthermore, supply chain management or JIT within the automotive industry on the other hand is showing a destruction of classical value chains. Suppliers are integrated within the production process and now deliver components more than mere parts.[4] The Automotive Network eXchange (ANX) from the U.S. is a further example of linking manufacturers with suppliers.[5]

Körner makes similar statements on the development of the insurance industry. The insurance market of the future will be a networked industry where customers have multiple access to insurance via the internet. Active and sophisticated customers will be able to make price comparisons via an internet broker. Low entry barriers will increase

---

[1] Szyperski/Klein (1999), www.uni-koeln.de/wiso-fak/veroeffentlichungen/e-commerce.htm
[2] www://bank24.de
[3] www://advance-bank.de
[4] Scheit (1999), pp. 121
[5] Evans/Wurster (1997), p. 32

the number of players and, as a result of that, companies will have to concentrate on their core competencies. The whole value chain will be covered by different providers.[1]

To sum up, it can be said that all the examples mentioned above come from so called mature industries and underpin Grant's statement that in mature industries the KSF revolve around process innovation and cost-efficiency scales (see page10).

4.4 Competitive advantage

According to Grant, competitive advantage is the capability to outperform rivals whereas the means applied or goals to be reached can be different but have the same object – to stay ahead of competitors.[2] He is of the opinion that competitive advantage arises when a company is able to tune its capabilities with its industry KSF's into a strategy. Organisational capabilities arise from a company's resources whereas the KSF's depend very much on the maturity of the industry.[3] The impact of increased international competition, economic turbulence and process innovation on mature industries creates a need for not just being efficient but also being able to quickly adjust to change and find new sources of innovation and differentiation.[4]

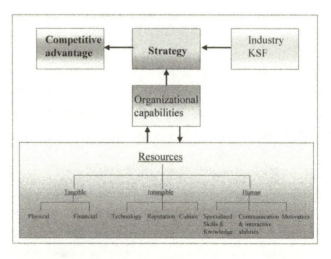

FIGURE 11: COMPETITIVE ADVANTAGE (GRANT 1995; P. 121)

---

[1] Körner (1999), p. 66
[2] Grant (1996), p. 151
[3] Grant (1996), pp. 294
[4] Grant (1996), p. 310

Michael E. Porter identified three main areas - what he calls *"generic strategies"* - in which a company can gain competitive advantage:[1]

- Cost (being cheaper or more efficient)
- Differentiation (being unique/quality)
- Focus (on cost or on differentiation)

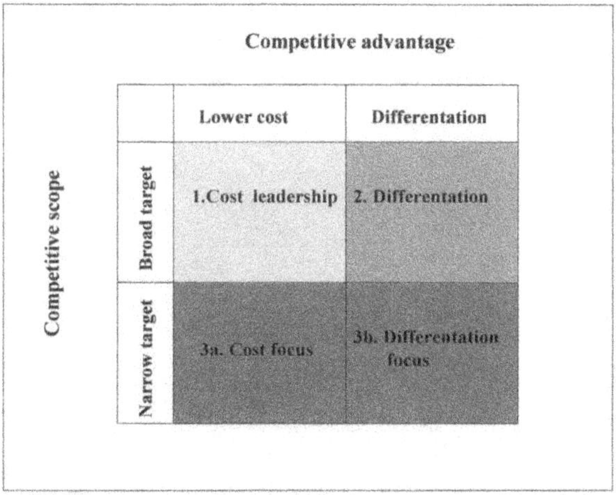

FIGURE 12: PORTER'S GENERIC STRATEGIES

However, according to Weiber and Kollmann the generic strategies of cost and quality leadership can be regarded as proven success factors in the last decades but in the recent past two other success factors have been identified: *time (speed) and flexibility.*[2] These two factors do not replace quality and cost but have to be added as a consequence of increased market dynamism and shorter product lifecycles. In addition, Kirzner found that competitive advantage in most cases has its origin in information advantage.[3] This success factor is justified since the production, processing and transformation of information increases efficiency and the effectiveness of business activities.[4] In addition to the two dimensions, quality-leadership and cost-leadership within the marketplace, the marketspace has two new dimensions, speed-leadership (fast production/extraction

---

[1] Porter (1985),pp. 11-16
[2] Weiber/Kollmann (1999), p. 52
[3] Weiber/Kollmann (1999), p. 52
[4] Weiber/ Jacob (1995), p. 513

of information) and topical-leadership (quality leader that produces or extracts high quality information).[1]

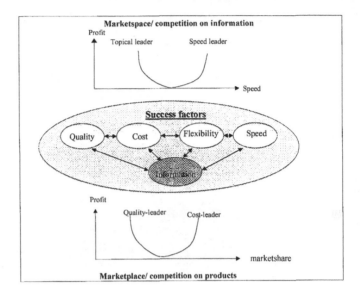

FIGURE 13: SUCCESS FACTORS (WEIBER/ KOLLMANN 1999, P. 59)

As already mentioned in chapter 4.4 transaction costs are extremely low with electronic commerce and, as a result of that, web-oriented companies will focus on core competencies.[2]

Hagel and Singer however, state that any company can be divided into three main businesses:

- management of customer relations,
- product innovation,
- management of infrastructure

These core businesses are not represented by business divisions but by "core business processes" that can extend from suppliers to the customers. However, rules that are underlying these three processes are in conflict with each other. Each process has its own laws and requires its own environment (company culture, -structure; skills etc.).

---

[1] Weiber/Kollmann (1999), p. 60
[2] Hagel/Singer (1999), p. 60

Bundling these three processes under one roof inevitably forces management to make compromises and results cannot be improved by reengineering and, as a consequence, the classical organisation has to be re-organised.[1]

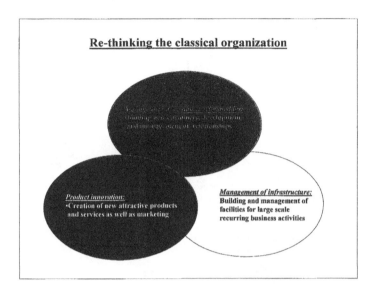

FIGURE 14: RETHINKING THE CLASSICAL ORGANISATION (FOLLOWING HAGEL/SINGER 1999; P. 62)

A similar development can be seen within the automotive industry where car manufacturers concentrate on core competencies, R & D, production, sales and service.[2]

Siebel and House are of the opinion that electronic commerce means the end of vertical integration and the rise of a new model called virtual integration.[3] In a dynamic and complex mature environment "continued success must be leveraged against interlocking resources."[4]

To sum up, the main changes or potentials to create competitive advantage through electronic commerce can be depicted with a figure taken from Sauter.[5]

---

[1] Hagel/Singer (1999), p. 62
[2] Scheit (1999),p. 121-122
[3] Siebel/House (1999), p. 86
[4] Siebel/House (1999), p. 86
[5] Sauter (1999), p. 103

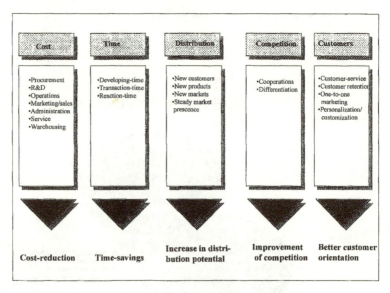

FIGURE 15: ELECTRONIC COMMERCE BENEFITS (SAUTER 1999, P. 103)

Sauter justifies these benefits the following way:

Costs:

Transaction costs can be reduced along the whole value chain (primary and support activities). Savings are estimated by reductions within sales of 40-60 % in the P & C field and 60-85% in personal insurance[1]. Main areas of cost reduction mentioned by Koch and Wagner are "paperlogistics", elimination of double work related to media breaks and the speeding up of information retrieval.[2]

Time savings (time-to-market):

Electronic commerce enables a dramatic reduction in processing time, reaction time to enquiries/complaints, product development etc.. In claim settlement savings are estimated at 75% in time.[3]

---

[1] Bechmann (1998), p. 1257
[2] Koch/Wagner (1999), p. 1496
[3] Gabor (1999), p. 519

Increase in market potential:
Electronic commerce opens up new customer segments and makes it easier to develop international markets. "Around-the-clock availability" is likely to increase turnover.[1]

Improvement of competitive situation/positioning:
Through co-operation and virtual networks a lot of companies find it much easier to complement their core competencies in order to strengthen their strategic situation. Virtual organisations are based on fast and smooth information interchange between partners. Furthermore, electronic commerce applications offer new products/services enabling differentiation from competitors.

Improvement in customer-orientation:
Improvements in customer-orientation can be made in two areas, customer service and personalisation of products and services. Customer satisfaction and thus customer retention can be increased by offering additional customer service based on electronic commerce. The same effect can be reached with "tailored" products/services via one-to-one marketing.

With the internet customers are better informed and thus have more power. The internet provides an infrastructure that allows not only the acceleration of processes but also cost reductions all along the value chain. The author is of the opinion that in such a dynamic environment companies will have to concentrate on the processes outlined by Hagel and Singer in order to perform well.

---

[1] Sauter (1999), p. 104

4.5   Business processes within the insurance industry

The insurance industry, which belongs to the service sector, has the main duty of securing human existence against different threats of life by averting disadvantages through the coverage of cash-requirements which arise as a consequence of a damage.[1] Based on this premise, two main operating processes can be deducted:

- the process of claim settling
- the process of policy issuing (as a certificate for coverage)

However, a lot of different players and sub-processes are involved in these core processes. Following Körner[2], the author would like to give a rough impression of the complexity of producing coverage with the following figure.

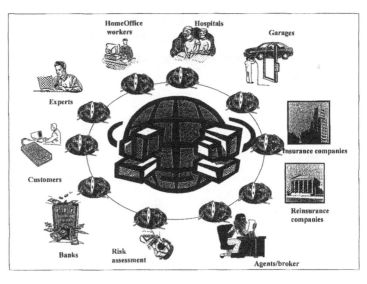

FIGURE 16: PLAYERS WITHIN THE INSURANCE INDUSTRY

According to the classification of electronic commerce outlined in chapter 3.2 the B2B area can be defined as the electronic settlement of business processes between companies whereas the B2C area focuses upon the end customer.[3]

---

[1] Büchner/ Winter (1986), p 10
[2] Körner (1999), p. 69
[3] Rohrbach (1999), pp. 272

Rohrbach states that the most important difference between the B2B and the B2C approach is the higher degree of complexity of the B2B approach which he explains with the following characteristics.

Issue	Characteristics
Relationship	Much more complex pricing business relationship can be seen: 1:1 in B2B and 1:n in B2C
Transactions	B2B normally requires a connection between different ERP systems
Strategic focus	B2B is normally focusing upon an improvement of the value chain whereas in the B2C field the aim is elimination of intermediaries.
Customer benefit	B2B concentrates on optimisation of business processes whereas B2C is connected to convenience and personalisation during the buying process

FIGURE 17: DIFFERENCES BETWEEN B2B AND B2C ELECTRONIC COMMERCE

Business-to-business opportunities within the insurance industry

As already mentioned above the business-to-business area of electronic commerce is focusing mainly on the improvement of co-operation between companies that are involved along the value chain[1]. As many studies predict, the B2B area will be the strongest driving factor for electronic commerce and not as formerly assumed the B2C area.[2] According to Kurz and Ortwein four characteristic B2B-relationships exist which distinguish between who is the driving force within the network: buyer, seller, intermediary or an integrated solution between two partners.[3]

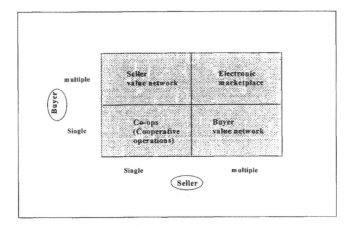

FIGURE 18: B2B-STRATEGIES

---

[1] Baumann (1999), p. 287
[2] OECD (1998), pp. 34 – 49
[3] Kurz/Ortwein (1999), p.131

However, the business processes within the insurance industry are quite different from retail or manufacturing industries, since there are no logistics, raw-materials or stocks to be managed. Depicting business processes and relationships in the business-to-business field for the insurance market depends very much on the insurance lines a company is operating. However, the following main relationships and processes can be identified.

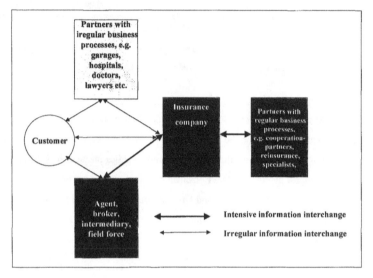

FIGURE 19: B2B PROCESSES WITHIN THE GERMAN INSURANCE INDUSTRY

The processes can be further divided into those where regular business transactions occur and those where irregular business transactions take place. In Kurz and Ortweins' terms the insurance company would be placed within the co-ops and the seller value network.

With reference to the business-to-business field within the insurance industry, the literature mainly focuses on the following issues:

- improvement of information and communication processes between co-operation partners[1] (intermediaries),
- transformation of business processes from intermediaries (broker, agents) to the point of sale[2] (policy issuing, claim settlement, contract information) in order to eliminate double work

As far as intermediaries or salespersons are concerned, information management and thus effectiveness play a major role. According to Siebel/Malone the informed salesforce needs instant access to relevant product data, competitors' products, brochures etc. in order to be able to make decisions on the spot - which in turn creates satisfied customers.[3] The main duty of sales information systems (or salesforce automation SFA) is to support salespeople with their work, e.g. planning, co-ordination, control and conduct of sales activities.

However, there are a lot more partners involved with both key processes mentioned earlier in this paragraph (see figure 16), e.g. hospitals, experts, garages, risk assessment by experts, administration etc.. All communication and information processes can be handled via internet.

Business-to-consumer processes within the insurance industry:

The internet will replace intermediaries and therefore comprise all processes concerning distribution and marketing and service or customer relationship management between insurance company and end customer.[4] Therefore it can be counted as classical direct marketing or sales and represents no new idea. However, Garvenand Wright are of the opinion that the intermediaries will not be removed - the old middleman (e.g. direct agent) will vanish and new middleman will emerge (e.g. Internetbroker).[5] The BCG is of the opinion that the internet will be established as an additional sales channel in the short and midterm. However, in the long term the internet will prevail over the

---

[1] Koch/Wagner (1998), p. 1721
[2] Kasten (1997), pp. 1091
[3] Siebel/Malone (1996), pp.16
[4] Bechmann (1998), p.1254
[5] Garven/Wright (1998), p. 5

traditional ones and new players and intermediaries (cybermediaries, software) will emerge[1].

The business processes with reference to the customers are:[2]

- Product information
- Communication / consulting
- Contract changes
- Advice services
- Claim settlement
- Personal calculations (presales phase)
- Sales (completion of contract)

A study from Datamonitor estimates that online-selling cuts administration and sales costs by 50% in addition to commissions saved.[3] Requirements for online distribution are:[4]

- Suitability of the product for online selling (see chapter 3. 1)
- Access to customers
- Appropriate pricing
- Fast handling of processes (delivery)
- Customer accepted payment methods

A new development has been identified in marketing. The emergence of increasing heterogenity among customers expectations and desires has resulted in personalised or customised products being offered.[5]

[1] Schwarz/Freese/Jacques (1999), pp. 1500-1504
[2] Gabor (1998), p. 515
[3] Gabor (1998), p. 517
[4] Köhler (1997), p. 43-44
[5] Fink (1998), p. 138

4.6 Organisational implications for electronic commerce

As already mentioned in the chapters earlier, the internet and with that electronic commerce has characteristics that influence current industry structures, business processes and also the organisation itself. With the help of the McKinsey 7 S-model, which is a proven tool for tuning an organisation (holistically) for success, the author would like to work out the areas affected by electronic commerce.

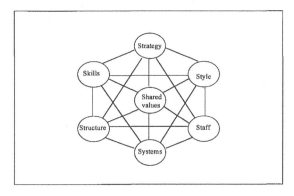

FIGURE 20: THE MCKINSEY 7 S- MODEL (PETERS/WATERMAN 1982, P. 32)

1. *Strategy*

According to Andersen Consulting the company's strategy has to become "eCommerce enlightened"[1], which means that electronic commerce activities have to be brought into alignment with the overall business goals of the company. Generally speaking, no internet concept should be implemented without a strategy. That way bad investment in IT-architecture and systems can be prevented, organisational implications can be taken into account and coherence with the overall business strategy be guaranteed.[2]

2. *Structure*

The adjustment of the organisation structure may be the most challenging part of electronic commerce since EC is growing very fast and has cross functional tasks and therefore affects established organisation as well as the company culture.[1] The reengineering of business processes and destruction of common value chains requires

---

[1] Andersen Consulting (1999), http://www.ac.com(showcase/ecommerce/ecom_whats_the_value.html
[2] Schwarz/Freese/Jacques (1999), p. 1504

new organisational structures. Evans and Wurster state that with the traditional trade-off of interactivity and reach of information, hierarchies are no longer necessary[2]. Flat organisational structures are necessary in order to speed up decisions and not only processes. Preis and Heinemann furthermore state, that the whole value chain has to be totally tuned to a customer focus so that the customer is able to serve himself and interact with the company on a 24/7 basis.[3] Seybold even found that companies that have successfully implemented e-commerce started reengineering their business processes from the customers point of view (360 °-approach).[4] This fact should normally be the most natural thing in developing buyer markets but, as so often, practice is lagging behind theory in this case.

3. *Staff*

Experiences from other industries such as finance and banking have shown that the implementation of modern technology such as ATM's and online-banking has reduced the numbers of staff and subsidiaries. But EC does not only affect inhouse staff but also the fieldforce whose role has to be newly defined for the forthcoming years.[5] However, experts also state that in the long term perspective EC will also create new jobs as new business models appear.[6]

4. *Skills*

If EC is to change industry structures and business rules it will also cause changes in the skills of staff. According to the OECD, EC requires a multi-skilled work-force that has IT-expertise as well as strong business application skills.[7] Additionally, skills are required that enable the workforce to perform business activities online. Because of the customer focus and increasingly well informed and demanding customers (24/7), staff should be able to serve customers satisfactorily.[8]

---

[1] Eggenberger/Klein (1999), p. 180
[2] Evans/Wurster (1997), p. 19-22
[3] Preis/Heinemann (1999), p. 126
[4] Seybold (1998), p 33-38
[5] Ulhaas/Scharek (1999), p. 4
[6] OECD (1998), p.17
[7] OECD (1998), p.18
[8] Eggenberger/Klein/Köchli/Lüthi (1999), pp. 132

5. *Systems*

The digitalisation of business processes should not end at a company's web server. Business processes also have to be handled electronically. Intranet, workflow, imaging and e-mail are imperatives for electronic commerce. [1] Seybold states that building a comprehensive and evolving e-business architecture will be a major source for doing business over the internet successfully .[2]

As mentioned earlier in chapter 4.1 EC is about reengineering and depicting business processes electronically and that requires that IT systems should be able to interact with any other in order to avoid media breaks and speed-up or reduce business processes costs respectively .[3] So the connection between back- and front-office systems as well as systems from other business partners represents a great challenge for successful e-commerce strategy implementation. Additionally, IT-systems must be able to handle personalised or customised products and services in order to correspond to customers' requirements.[4]

6. *Shared values*

The author is of the opinion that the style and culture of a company depend very much on its strategic positioning. However, owing to the customer-focused business approach characteristic of EC, as already outlined earlier in this dissertation, the staff need to be consequently customer oriented. Additionally, the style or culture should be characterised by entrepreneurial thinking rather than by the bureaucratic and hierarchical aspects common amongst German insurance companies. Even today it is still possible to find a hierarcy of titles whose names such as "Inspector" or "Headinspector" are more reminiscent of a tax department than a dynamic, customer focused and networked insurance company.

---

[1] Baumann /Kirstner (1999), pp. 301
[2] Seybold (1998), p. 6
[3] Hess (1999), p. 187
[4] E-Business Technology Forecast (1999), p. 44

7. *Style*

Baumann and Kirstner are of the opinion that a participative leadership style is an imperative for implementing EC within an organisation because autocratic determined managers would prevent the organisational development process.[1]

4.7 Success factors for Electronic commerce

With regard to the success factors for electronic commerce the literature distinguishes between the factors that have to be taken into account on the operational side, e.g. managing a web-site, as well as on the strategic side which can be divided into technological issues (B2B), marketing issues (B2C) as well as in organizational issues.[2] Due to the conceptual focus of this dissertation the author will focus on the strategic area.

Electronic commerce aspects

- For the B2B area the integration of business partners into the initiative has proven very successful.[3]
- The deconstruction of existing value chains combined with a consequent focus on customer requirements has been an outstanding characteristic of successful EC companies. Dell and Cisco with their excellent supply-chain management are examples of this.[4]
- A consequent focus on end customers regarding products and services and business processes (360 ° degee approach) has proven to be a success factor within the B2C field of electronic commerce.[5]
- Following the rules of one-to one-marketing: treating customers according to their preferences and desires (customizing of products and services/CRM).[6]

---

[1] Baumann/Kistner (1999), p. 442
[2] Priess/Heinemann (1999), p. 120-125
[3] PricewaterhouseCoopers (1999), p. 6
[4] Priess/Heinemann (1999), p. 125
[5] Seybold (1998), p. 6
[6] Priess/Heinemann (1999), p. 123

Organisational aspects:

As far as organisational issues are concerned, the following success factors are mentioned [1]:

- E-Commerce has to be business and not IT driven
- Company culture and change has to be taken into account
- All inhouse operations and the entire organizational structure has to be taken into account when doing electronic commerce[2]
- Senior management should be committed and the key driver for doing electronic commerce.[3]

To sum up it can be argued that in order to be successful at electronic commerce the whole organisation has to be adusted to new business processes that are fully customer oriented.

4.8 Summary of literature research

The review of literature on the subject has revealed that the German insurance industry is in the middle of restructuring after a long period of regulation and owing to increased competition. Cost pressure is forcing insurance companies to cut costs and reengineer business processes by deploying modern IT systems in order to satisfy sophisticated and price-performance oriented customers.

Electronic commerce is expected to sky rocket in the coming years since it not only provides time, cost and differentiation advantages but is regarded as providing access to an increasing number of online users too. The driving force for EC will be the business-to-business area.

The investigation of products and services has shown that the suitability of insurance products depends on their complexity and specific demand (e.g. car insurance). In general it can be said that the standardised products of the private customer segment are well suited for online sales.

---

[1] PricewaterhouseCoopers (1999), p. 6
[2] Schreiber (1998), p. 59
[3] PricewaterhouseCoopers (1999), p.6

As a consequence of reduced transaction costs and increasing competition companies will have to concentrate more and more on core competencies in order to create competitive advantage. As a result of that, traditional value chains are likely to change which in turn results in changes to the structure of the industry with new rules and new CSF's. This development is most likely to occur within mature industries where cost-efficiency scales and process innovation have become KSF's. This trend has already been seen to emerge in other mature industries such as the automobile industry.

Electronic commerce has been proven to provide competitive advantage in a lot of areas such as providing cost - and time savings from lean processes both in the B2B and the B2C field, or as a distribution channel and through better customer service. Additionally, the general economic trend from mass markets towards tailored products and services is seen to be ideally implemented by electronic commerce and modern IT solutions.

However, it is clear that electronic commerce is not only about IT, procurement and sales processes but implies a consequent alignment of the whole organisational structure and inhouse processes if it is to be applied successfully.

The following table provides an overview of the authors quoted and a brief summary of their findings:

Author	Key findings
Albers Sönke, Clement Michael, Peters Kay Skiera Bernd	Development of electronic commerce, perspectives,
Andersen Consulting	EC and strategy, impact of EC on enterprises, markets and economies
Baumann Martina, Kistner Andreas	Definitions od EC and e-business, General overview on EC and e-business, leadership within EC, organisational impacts
Bechmann Torsten	Perspectives of Ecand the insurance industry, trends in EC
Berryman Kenneth, Harrington Lorraine, Layton-Rodin Dennis, Rerolle Vincent	Types of electronic marketplaces, opportunities for marketplaces, factors for development of electronic markets
Bliemel Friedhelm, Fassot Georg, Theobald Axel	Definition of EC, characteristics of EC, growth expectations,

Eggenberger Christian, Klein Stefan	Organisational implications of EC, business processes,
Eggenberger Christian, Klein Stefan Köchli Susanne, Lüthi Ursula	Implications for the workforce within EC; social aspects, human resources,
Evans Philip B. Wurster Thomas S.	Destruction of value chains, change of organisations and industry structures, EC and its implications for competitive advantage
Fink Dietmar H.	Marketing strategies, customisation,
Gabor Andreas	EC strategies for insurance companies, online sales channel, benefits of EC
Garven James R. Wright William H.	Impact of EC on insurance industry, role of intermediaries, internet trends for insurance,
Grant Robert M.	Strategic implications, competeitive advantage,
Hagel John, Singer Marc	Concentration on one of three core business processes; global development of industry structures, networked economy, transaction costs,destruction of traditional value chains
Hermanns Arnold	Impacts and challenges of electronic commerce
Hermanns Arnold, Sauter Michael	Definitions of EC, areas and examples of EC,
Hünerberg Reinhard, Mann Andreas	Online service- examples and functions
Kasten Hans H.	Business processes within the German insurance industry,
Koch Gottfried, Wagner Fred	General implications and perspectives of EC within the German insurance industry, virtual organizations, cooperations between insurers and banks in EC, service aspects
Köhler Thomas	Setting up online saleschannel,
Körner Jochen	Impact of the internet on insurance industry, future scenarios, trends
Kühlmann Knut Kurtenbach W. Käßler-Pawelka Günter	Marketing aspects of the German insurance industry
Kurz Eberhard, Ortwein Eckard	EC strategies within the B2B area, business networks,
Magheiro Lynn Henry Dave, Cooke Sandra, Montes Sabrina	Impact of the internet on the economy, impact on different industries, case studies
Muther Andreas	CRM and IT, information age
OECD study	Economic and social impact of EC, skills and jobs,
Peppers Don, Rogers Martha	The principle of one-to-one marketing (mass customisation).
Peters Kay, Clement Michel	Development of EC, estimations and perspectives, definitions of EC
Peters Thomas J., Waterman Robert H.	7 S- framework, organisational success factors
Porter Michael E.	Generic strategies, creation of competitive advantage.
Price WaterhouseCoopers	Impact of e-business on economy and several industries, benefits of EC a

Priess Stefan Heinemann Christopher	Success factors for electronic commerce, B2B and B2C field of EC
Rayport Jeffrey R. Sviokla John J.	Virtual value chains, competitive advantage,
Rohrbach Peter	EC within the B2B field, concepts and strategies, technical aspectsof EC
Sauter Michael	Destruction of Value chains, change of industry structures,
Scheit Alexander	Implications of EC for automovive industry, trends, supply chain management
Schinzer Heiko	Suitability of products and services for EC, EC and value creation
Schinzer Heiko, Thome Rainer	Definition of EC, scenarios of EC as well as IT-players within EC market
Schreiber Gerhard Andreas	Success factors for EC, staff requirements, business models
Schwarz Gunther Freese Christopher, Christioph Jacques	Trategic options of insurance companies within EC, success factors for EC, strategic considerations
Seybold Patricia B.	Internet business strategies, CSF for EC, case studies and best practice examples
Siebel Thomas M., Malone Michael	Need for Total sales quality, CRM; reengineering of sales processes
Siebel Thomas M., House Pat	Best practice examples of EC, success factors for EC strategies, virtual value chains, custumerisation,
Szyperski Norbert, Klein Stefan	Reference-model for EC, value chain, classification of EC, perspectives, options
Ulhaas Wolfgang, Scharek Bernhard	Impact of EC on insurance industry, sales channels, business processes
Weiber Rolf, Kollmann Tobias	Virtual an physical value chains, value creation and competitive advantage, role of information, competitive strategies

FIGURE 21: SUMMARY TABLE OF AUTHORS AND THEIR KEYFINDINGS

5 Fieldwork

5.1 Research and objectives

Fieldwork was carried out within the scope of this dissertation . The objectives of the fieldwork were to get empirical evidence on the hyphothesis addressed and to compare this on a theoretical level with the literature review. The purpose of the fieldwork was to provide a general overview of the subject of electronic commerce within the German insurance industry, i.e. how they think about the development of the German insurance market, what they think about electronic commerce and what are their current and planned activities in terms of electronic commerce. The overall issue of the research was to find out whether insurance companies think that they can create competitive advantage using electronic commerce and how they are going to realise or plann it.

Based on the results of the fieldwork an analysis and comparison with the findings from the literature review shall be carried out in order to reveal correlations or gaps between theory and practice.

Finally, the author would like to make recommendations about the deployment of Electronic commerce amongst German insurance companies using the results of the analysis.

5.2 Methodology and scope - outline

The author decided for a combination of a mailed questionnaire and semi-structured interviews as methods for gathering data. The questionnaire fieldwork was carried out in order to get large samples at relatively low cost [1] with the intention of obtaining a general overview of the current status of and opinions about e-commerce within the German insurance industry, e.g. current thinking about electronic commerce, suitable products, suitable business processes, issues addressed etc.. In order to get insight into customers views concerning online-shopping and insurance the author fell back on secondary data. A present day study from w3B- Gruppe[2] which is specialised in internet

---

[1] Remenyi/Williams/Money/Swartz (1998), p. 156
[2] Fittkau & Maaß (1999)

user research in Germany was regarded as the most expressive. Therefore the author decided to undertake no study of his own in this regard.

In the course of this research the author realised that he had put no emphasis on the strategic focus, e.g. future development of industry, main future business drivers, implications and constraints etc. and decided to conduct additional interviews with CIO's.

In the scope of this fieldwork the author addressed a sample of 100 German insurance companies that approximately matches the composition of the German insurance market[1]: 27 life insurers, 12 health insurers and 61 P&C companies were addressed. Four companies were direct insurers and the remaining operated different sales channels such as direct agents, brokers, part-time agents and banks.

5.3 Questionnaire on e-commerce

The questionnaire was divided into two main sections, a general part that was designed to get information on company size, business and insurance lines and sales channels operated as well as information about the person answering, and an e-commerce part asking questions on specific areas of e-commerce and the insurance industry. The questionnaire consists of 26 questions addressing the following subjects.[2]

1. How does the German insurance industry think about the internet as a sales channel?
2. Which products and services are suitable for distribution over the internet?
3. Which impact does e-commerce have on the business processes and the strategic alignment of insurance companies?
4. What business processes are suitable for depiction or support with e-commerce?
5. What do they think about creating competitive advantage with electronic commerce?
6. How do insurers adapt to the age of the internet and what are their plans and actions already undertaken?
7. Where are the constraints in implementing e-commerce within an insurance company?

[1] Statistical Yearbook (1998), p. 36
[2] Questionnaire see Appendix 3, p. 64

5.4   Interviews with CIO'S

The purpose of the interviews was to get more insight into strategic issues such as changes within the industry structure, strategies and organisational issues. The author conducted semi structured interviews for this purpose.[1] It proved to be very difficult to get in touch with senior managers and therefore the author could only conduct four interviews. The interview partners were CIO's from mid-size companies mainly engaged in the private customer section. With reference to sales channels, each of the classical distribution channels; direct- sales, brokers and part-time agents was represented. The questions asked revolved around the following issues:

1) E-commerce and its impact on traditional value chains?
2) Changing determinants of competition (5 forces; PEST, key drivers)?
3) How can insurance companies create competitive advantage deploying electronic commerce?
4) What are the critical success factors for insurance companies?
5) What strategies will be successful?
6) Which scenarios are likely to occur in the B2B field?

5.5   Limitations of the research

As mentioned earlier only 15 interviewees disclosed their identities as senior managers. 8 can be counted to the 2nd managerial level and the rest of the respondents declared the division they worked in but did not say anything about their position within the company. The author therefore sees the following limitations of the fieldwork:

- The questionnaire might be answered by middle managers who are not that familiar with strategic planning and thinking.
- The answers do not fully reflect the thinking and planning of senior managers on electronic commerce.
- Because of the great number of IT people who responded the questions on strategic alignment and competitive advantage might not be answered carefully due to the lack of economic background (basic models, concepts).

Therefore the author decided to draw back on secondary research data from other research projects carried out by consultancy companies such as Price Waterhouse

[1] Interview guide see Appendix 4 p. 69

Coopers, Andersen Consulting and McKinsey on the financial service industry including insurance and other industries in Europe and the U.S.. With that approach the author wanted to evaluate the validity of the primary data gathered.

6   Findings and analysis of Fieldwork Data

6.1   General findings

33 out of 100 replied which corresponds to a return rate of 33%. This ratio can be regarded as outstandingly high and reflects the current relative importanceof electronic commerce amongst German insurers. The questionnaire was addressed to the board of directors, however only 15 respondents indicated their position as a senior manager. 8 can be counted to the 2nd managerial level and the rest made no statement on that question. Very interesting is the fact that 55 % of the respondents came from the IT department and 24% from the sales division. The rest is split up between administration, public relations and marketing (see figure below).

Department	Amount	Percent
Marketing	3	9%
Sales	8	24%
PR	2	6%
IT	18	55%
Administration	2	6%
Total	33	100%

FIGURE 22: PROFESSIONAL BACKGROUND OF RESPONDENTS

This can be interpreted as a first indicator of how the e-commerce issue is placed within German insurance companies and with which general point-of-view the subject of electronic commerce and of course problem-solving is tackled.

However this result is not extraordinary. A study from Forrester Research on electronic commerce projects found that "IT staff and consultants – not business people, customers, or trading partners - make up the bulk of the project teams enabling these new business connections."[1]

---

[1] Cameron/Deutsch/Walker/Hermsdorf (1999), http://www.forrester.com Driving IT's Externalisation, p.5

An average team consists of the following team-members:

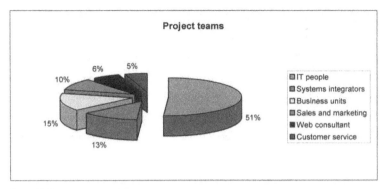

The author wanted to get an overview of the different sales channels German insurance companies are operating epecially to which extent the sales channel internet is already in place. The questionaire revealed the following results:

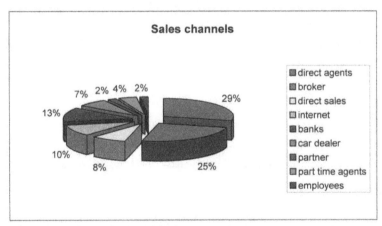

About 10 % stated that they are already operating the internet as a sales channel. However, the interviews have shown that the companies that stated that they would operate the internet as a sales channel do not offer online insurance so far. Contracts are still concluded via mail or fax. The German Federal Insurance Supervisory Office does not accept online insurance owing to legal doubts.[1]

---

[1] Schwarz/Freese/Jacques(1999), p. 1503 and Lier (1999), p. 1488

6.2   Future industry trends

In order to match the CSFs that have to be taken into account for the creation of competitive advantage the CIOs were asked about the main influences (from the macro- and micro environment) and trends influencing the insurance industry. Owing to the low number of interviews the author was only able to identify the main trends and influences foreseen by senior managers. The author is of the opinion that ranking the answers would not be very expressive. Therefore the author fell back on secondary data in this field. The senior managers who were questioned expect the following trends and influences on the German insurance industry, mainly as a result of the internet.

1.   Sophisticated and demanding customers

Customers will increasingly move towards online insurance in the private customer segment in the next 10 years. Intermediaries will be reduced in the following years but will exist in the future as well. Owing to this expected development, insurance products will change dramatically. More simple and modular insurance products will emerge. Two CIO's are expecting that the classical insurance lines will vanish and personally tailored coverage over several business lines are going to emerge. They could imagine that within the next 10-15 years a "Frank Berger" policy for example will exist.

2.   Technology

Technology will enable insurance companies to automate and reengineer operating processes so that fewer intermediaries and inhouse staff will be involved along the entire value chain. In short, technology will reduce operating costs on account of the fewer staff (inhouse and field) needed.

Furthermore, IT will become a major success factor in the future not only because of the reduction in operating costs but also in coupling different sales channels such as the telephone and the world wide web.

Similar findings were made by Forrester Research in a study of U.S insurance companies. Senior managers expect that sales channels such as the internet, call-centers and agents will interact with each other and therefore net influenced sales will increase.[1]

---

[1] Forrester Research (1999), http://www.forrester.com

3. Competitors

New competitors will emerge, especially new internet insurance companies that will start as newcomers. Additionally, banks, who are are seen as a main threat for the classical insurance company, will move stronger into the insurance business as online insurers because of their excellent position, having already established a foothold in the internet business through online-banking.

This statement is underpinned by a study by Mummert & Partner who argue that a lot of insurance companies think about founding new subsidiaries to focus on online insurance.[1]

4. Industry structure:

The CIO's questioned stated that they expect that the German insurance industry will dramatically change within the next 10-15 years. Three out of four were of the opinion that the standardised private customer segment will almost completely migrate to the internet sales channel, maybe in connection with call centers. Similar findings were made by Forrester Research in a study amongst U.S. insurance companies. Senior managers expect that sales channels will interact with each other e.g. internet, call-center and agents and therefore net influenced sales will increase.[2]

Another expected development in this case is that some insurance lines are expected to move into other industries such as car insurance which is expected to move into the automotive industry.

Personal customer contact or the classical sales organisations (direct agents, broker, etc.) will not become extinct. However they will be reduced dramatically and concentrate on more complex issues, e.g. commercial, industrial sector.
A study from Andersen Consulting who investigated the influence of the internet on current sales channels underpins this assessment (see figure 25).[3]

---

[1] Mummert & Partner (1999), http://www.mummert.de/deutsch/press/990509.html
[2] Forrester Research (1999), http://www.forrester.com
[3] Wetzel (1998), p. 256

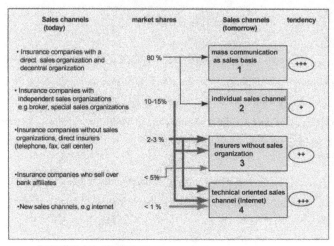

FIGURE 25: CHANGE IN SALES CHANNELS

6.3 Consumer profiles, expectations and behaviour

Customer data especially about their attitudes towards electronic commerce, their behaviour and preferences for products and services is quite important for a company's EC-strategy and the creation of competitive advantage.

As mentioned earlier these data are taken from a study by w3B[1] who is specialised in investigating the profile and behaviour of German internet users.

This survey revealed the following main socio-democratic trends:

> ➢ Level of education approaches population average
> ➢ Female users have increased exponentially over the last four years. With a share of 23,5% in 1999 almost every fourth user in Germany is a woman.
> ➢ The age-pyramid is getting flatter, i.e. the increase of younger - (under 20) as well as the older - (over 50) user is proportionally stronger compared to the other age groups. The 20-29 year old age group has decreased from 68 % in 1995 to 35 % in 1999.
> ➢ The number of students has decreased from 40.4% in 1996 to 14.2% in 1999 whereas the number of employees and freelancers has increased.

socio-democratic trends

feature	1996	1997	1998	1999
education				
no degree	29,8%	22,8%	21,8%	23,1%
apprenticeship	20,4%	25,0%	28,7%	32,4%
advanced technical college	10,8%	20,0%	20,1%	19,2%
university	26,7%	21,4%	19,7%	17,0%
promotion	4,7%	4,9%	4,3%	3,0%
other	7,6%	6,0%	5,4%	5,2%
age				
>50	2,8%	7,1%	10,7%	10,4%
40-49	8,2%	13,9%	15,5%	15,2%
30-39	28,5%	30,9%	31,0%	30,5%
20-29	56,1%	41,2%	35,3%	35,1%
<19	4,4%	6,9%	7,5%	8,7%
profession				
employee	30,0%	39,2%	43,6%	45,7%
free lancer	10,3%	14,9%	16,3%	14,2%
student	40,4%	22,4%	17,1%	15,0%
pupils	5,0%	7,7%	8,0%	10,8%
doctoral candidate	6,8%	3,7%	2,4%	1,7%
other	4,1%	7,1%	8,1%	8,2%

FIGURE 26: SOCIO-DEMOCRATIC TRENDS

---

[1] Fittkau/Maaß (1999), p.7-16

This analysis revealed that the internet is likely to become a mass medium like TV and radio. The results observed show that online users -from their socio-democratic profile- are approaching the population average more and more. Especially the rise in the numbers of employees and freelancers results in higher purchasing power for the internet population and thus it represents a more attractive target group.

With reference to the user behaviour the study from Fittkau & Maaß has found the following results:

Over 50% of the questioned internet users stated that the www is a good/very good medium for shopping with the main benefits of independence from opening hours, convenience, time-savings as well as easy ordering and price comparisons.[1] This is very important information when tackling a B2C strategy in order to achieve competitive advantage.

FIGURE 27: EVALUATION OF ONLINE-SHOPPING

However, with reference to the financial sector and especially the insurance industry the findings are not that euphorical. Only 24 % would and 9,6 % have already bought financial services online.

Product/service	would	have
music	60,9%	36,0%
books	68,3%	62,0%
studies/reports	20,9%	6,9%
software	67,1%	52,1%
computer hardware	41,7%	28,3%
furnitures	8,3%	3,6%
financial services, stocks, insurances	24,6%	9,6%
tickets (travel)	58,1%	21,6%
travel	41,1%	10,5%
tickets (entertainment)	53,8%	12,2%

FIGURE 28: PREFERRED PRODUCTS FOR ONLINE SHOPPING

---

[1] Appendix 5, p. 71

In the author's opinion this does not represent a refusal of online insurance since there
are not many possibilities for customers to purchase insurance online at the moment (see
fieldwork chapter 6.1). This result confirms in general the findings of the literature
review that both digital- and non-digital products from the low and mid-size price
segment are best suited for electronic commerce. Because of the growing interweaving
of banking (financial services) and the insurance industry both sections shall be looked
at in some detail.

Purchase of financial services

feature	in %
stocks/bonds	35,2%
fonds	21,8%
investment products	10,6%
financing (property)	4,4%
take out a loan	8,9%
building society savings agreement	6,0%
online-banking	61,1%
no financial services	31,1%

Purchase of insurance

feature	in %
motor third party insurance	26,2%
motor hull insurance	22,4%
health insurance	12,7%
accident insurance	11,8%
life-/pension insurance	10,5%
disability insurance	9,5%
personal liability insurance	16,4%
insurance on contents	16,5%
claim settlement	40,5%
none	51,4%

FIGURE 29: PRODUCTS/SERVICES FROM CUSTOMERS' POINT OF VIEW

As depicted in the figure above over half of the questioned internet users would not buy
insurance products or trade services over the internet. Of those people that would buy
products/services, car insurance and the non complex P & C products are favourites.
It is interesting to the author that health insurance is rated higher than life/pension
insurance.

To sum up, there is a clear trend within the financial industry towards online banking
and brokerage in the private customer segment. The reasons for this lie in the business
being more transaction-oriented and being on the web longer. Concerning the insurance
industry and the preferred products and services there is a clear trend towards the service
enhancing aspect of electronic commerce by handling claim settlement over the web.
The most preferred products are those that can already be called commodities: car
insurance, liability and accident insurance.

The author comes to the conclusion that the empirical findings substantiate the predictions that were made in the literature on the subject. If insurance companies are going to offer online insuring and if servicing is going to increase enormously in the private customer segment as predicted then this business is very likely to move into the sales channel internet.

6.4 Products and services

This data was gathered with the intention of balancing the views of literature, customers and insurers. The customer's view is especially important in terms of competitive advantage.

Products

The survey revealed that 80 % of the recipients find the internet a suitable medium for selling insurance. However, the answers concerning the suitable insurance lines differ and are to some extent surprising.

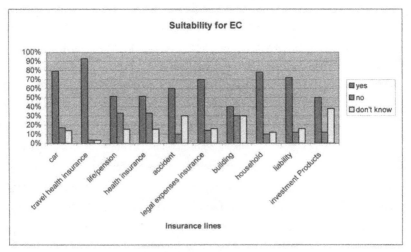

FIGURE 30: SUITABILITY OF INSURANCE PRODUCTS

Very astonishing is the fact that life/pension insurance is only rated with a suitability of 51.5% since at 80% this represents the greatest share of direct insurance business in Germany.[1] The interviews revealed that this question was formulated too globally. The interviewees stated that they could imagine selling risk life insurances, child's deferred assurances and simple life and pension insurance online but not mortgage insurance nor complex provisions for old age.

The other results are more or less congruent with the literature, that means the greater the complexity of the product the less suitable it is for electronic commerce. The P&C products were rated between 50 % and 90 % suitable for electronic commerce. Health and life/pensions and investment funds are seen twofold with ratings of around 50%. With reference to the investment funds the author is of the opinion that a lot of insurance companies do not offer these products and are not familiar with them. Otherwise they would have rated these products higher since online stocktrading is one of the most successful businesses within the financial sector.[2] To sum up, the standardised mass market products are seen to be most suitable for selling over the internet.

Linking these findings with the customers point of view outlined in the chapter before it can be stated that, in general, there is agreement about which products are suitable for electronic commerce between insurance companies, customers and the literature on the subject. The only deviation from this thesis is that customers rate health insurance higher than the literature and insurers. The author explains this finding with the above average educational level of online users even if there are signs that this is going to vanish as outlined in chapter 6.2.

[1] Datamonitor (1998), p. 1
[2] Siebel/House (1999), 27

Services

Concerning services, 100 % of the responses rated the internet as an appropriate medium for servicing customers. About 90 % of the questioned companies offer product and company information on the net. 56 % offer self help books and 40 % already offer claim announcement as well as personalised offers via the net. It is interesting that within the next 1-2 years about 50 % of the companies are planning to install online tracking of claim status and roughly the same amount will be able to handle online administrative changes.

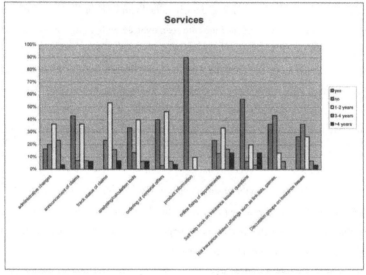

FIGURE 31: SERVICE OFFERINGS

Linking these results with the characteristics of online services outlined earlier it can be said that there is a great deal of convergence with the literature on the subject. It is obvious that in these days services prevail (product information, calculation, self-help-books/FAQ) that do not need any online connection to legacy systems. However, a look at activities planned for the future shows that these service and applications are likely to emerge pretty soon. Over 50% of the questioned companies are planning to install online tracking of claim status within the next 2 years.

6.5   Value chain and competitive advantage

The questionnaire and the interviews included the subject of value chains and the destruction of existing business processes. The questionnaire revealed the following result:

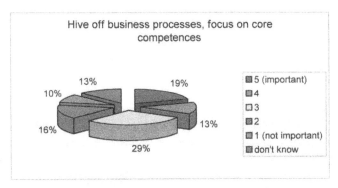

Only 19% rated this task at 5 (very important) and an additional 13% at 4 (important). Taking both ratings together around about a third of the persons questioned rated this point as at least important. This result differs widely from that what the literature is saying on the destruction of existing value chains owing to the reduction in transaction costs and the need for focusing on core competencies in order to create value in an increasingly competitive environment.

The interviews revealed a similar result. The CIO's did not think that destruction of current processes and focusing on core competencies is compelling. They think that the existing old processes can be kept under one hat if the processes are pruned lean. However, they did not reject the literature but admitted that this could make sense in some cases but definitely not in general. The thesis of Hagel and Singer - outlined in chapter 4.5 - was regarded as very theoretical. One CIO stated, that he expects new sales channels for some products, e.g. car insurance and car dealers but the classical value chain (see chapter 4.4) will remain as usual.

However, these answers are quite interesting since value chains in other mature industries such as automotive and retail banking are going to change significantly. JIT has changed the procurement side in the automotive industry and is, according to a study by Klein and Selz, in the middle of restructuring the sales side as virtual car dealers emerge.[1] On the other hand home banking is changing the banking industry on the distribution and administration side by cutting out bank subsidiaries.[2]

The answers and statements made it clear that today's insurance managers are focusing on cost reduction, streamlining current processes and providing additional customer service in order to gain competitive advantage. This impression is underpinned by a study from PWC on European companies from different industries that "for the most part they have not achieved the benefits to be derived from exploiting approaches that drive top-line revenue and those that add a new dimension to their businesses."[3]

One general question on the main benefits of electronic commerce was formulated as a multiple choice question. The respondents made the following choices.

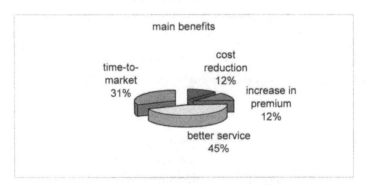

FIGURE 33: MAIN BENEFITS OF ELECTRONIC COMMERCE

There is a clear trend for the service enhancing aspect of electronic commerce at 45% followed by lean and faster processes (time-to-market) at approximately 33%. It is interesting that cost savings and increases in premium income play a minor role for the respondents. These results go along with the findings made by PWC in other industries;

---

[1] Klein/Selz (1999); p.1
[2] Evans/Wurster (1997), p. 32
[3] Electronic Business Outlook (1999), p. 22

that most CEO's think that they are seeking to find competitive advantage through premium service.[1] When one refers this result to the literature and what is said about mature industries there is an obvious mismatch. According to the literature, the KSF in mature industries are process innovation, buyer selection and cost-efficiency scales.[2]

With reference to the impact on the strategic alignment of the companies, 10 closed questions were asked on the options mentioned beneath. Respondents replied in order of importance as follows:

- Marketing   44%
- Additional sales channel with (online sales)   35%
- Development of new products   31%
- New sales channels (other industries)   29%
- Offer wider product range (differentation)   25%
- Specialisation on products (focus)   20%
- Focus on core competences   20%
- Fix new cooperations   16%
- Enter new markets; geographical (penetration)   13%

The entrance of new geographical markets at 13% was regarded as the least important factor for the strategic alignment of German insurance companies. The opinion about product development is very interesting. The replies are very balanced along the whole rating scale from 1 to 5. This is a sign to the author that there is no clear understanding about the role of products within electronic commerce and that differs widely from what the literature is saying about personalisation or customisation as a key factor of electronic commerce. The complete result is shown in figure 34.

[1] Electronic Business Outlook (1999), p. 14
[2] Grant (1996), p. 237

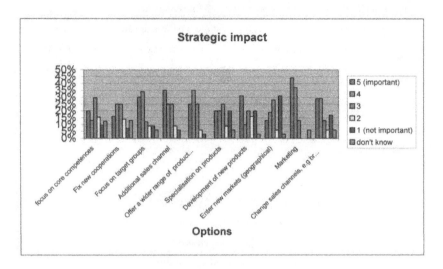

The question on competitive advantage was formulated as an open one. The question was focusing on whether the questioned persons think that electronic commerce provides competitive advantage for their companies and if so, in which areas. In short, the result was that 70 % said that electronic commerce would provide competitive advantage for their company, 23% said no, electronic commerce will not provide any competitive advantage; 7% did not know.

The reasons and the sectors in which electronic commerce is going to provide them with competitive advantage were very interesting. The answers are listed in figure 34.

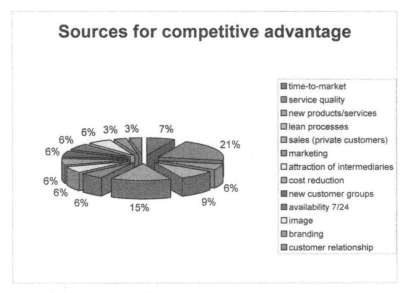

FIGURE 35: SOURCES OF COMPETITIVE ADVANTAGE

Of the respondents 21% chose service quality as a major source of competitive advantage followed by sales at 15% and lean processes at 9%.

Linking these statements to the sources of competitive advantage as defined by Hermans in paragraph 4.6 the statements can be grouped as follows:

Areas	Statements
Cost reduction	*Cost reduction*
Time savings	*Lean processes, time-to-market*
Distribution	*Sales, new customer groups*
Improvement of competition	*Attraction of intermediaries, image, branding*
Improvement in customer orientation	*Service quality, CRM, new products/services, availability*

FIGURE 36: LINKING OF STATEMENTS TO ELECTRONIC COMMERCE BENEFITS

It proved to be very difficult to clearly assign these areas to the outlined areas of electronic commerce since the statements could be assigned to several points. Lean processes for instance normally have an impact on costs and time savings.

However according to the author's classification the following assignment results:

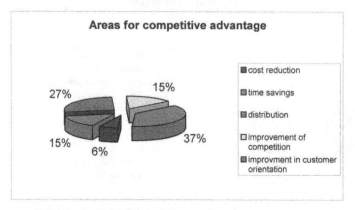

FIGURE 37: AREAS FOR COMPETITIVE ADVANTAGE- RESEARCH RESULT

The main area that is regarded as creating competitive advantage is improvement in customer orientation at 37% followed by distribution at 27%. Very interesting in this case is the fact that time-savings and especially cost reduction only play a minor role. Considering the maturity of this industry and the increased price/performance competition the author expected a much higher result in these areas. On the other hand this result does make a lot of sense since customer retention is a very important issue in saturated markets. Shorter contract cycles and increasing commoditization in the private customer segment decreases customers' switching costs and requires good customer relationships in order to keep customers.

The interviews revealed that some CIO's think that the only way to create competitive advantage is to found a new "Internet insurance company" with new products for the private customer segment with no other intermediary involved. This would be the only way to have success in the long run since operating a classical sales channel with intermediaries and the internet together in one company would cause trouble with the sales organisation. Companies that operate a sales organisation within the private customer segment will be out of business in the long run.

A similar finding was made by Mummert & Partner who identified a degree of polarisation between the internet as a sales channel and the classical sales channel "intermediaries" in the private customer segment.[1]

6.6 Business processes

In order to be able to make comparisons with the literature the author divided business processes into B2C and B2B areas just as they are treated in literature. It was the intention of the author to work out the business processes that are suitable for EC in order to achieve competitive advantage through cost advantages and satisfied customers through leaner and faster processes.

a) Business-to-consumer:

The questions on B2C processes were asked as multiple choice questions based on the current services offered by German insurance companies. Additionally, the interviewees had the possibility of adding services they think would be suitable for the net. The results were as follows:

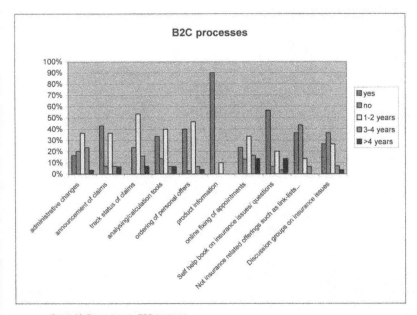

FIGURE 38: EVALUATION OF B2C PROCESSES

---

[1] Mummert & Partner (1999), http://www.mummert.de/

The business processes in the B2C field imply more or less the same sales and service issues as already mentioned in paragraph 6.2. There is a clear trend for information management and claim settlement (integration of customer, contract information). Additionally, the whole sales process is regarded as suitable for the internet - restricted to products for the private customer segment- as already mentioned in chapter 6.3. This result is totally in line with the theoretical statements of the first section of this dissertation.

b) *Business-to-Business*

In the B2B field the author concentrated on a few core processes an insurance company has to handle with its business partners. The main processes concern those related to intermediaries or sales organizations. However, there are of course "third parties" such as garages, lawyers, doctors hospitals, police etc. who are involved in delivering the insurance service mainly in loss situations or risk assessment. These business partners were a subject of the interviews with CIO's.

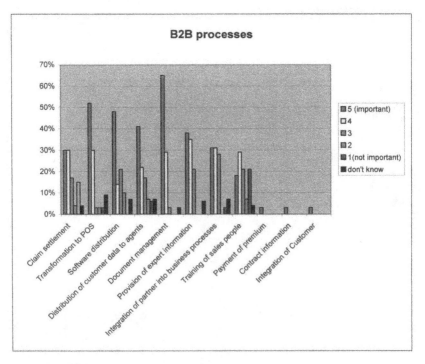

FIGURE 39: BUSINESS PROCESSES IN THE BUSINESS-TO-BUSINESS FIELD

The companies questioned rated the following processes as important (5):

1. Document management (documents on demand)   65%
2. Transformation of business processes to the POS   52%
3. Software distribution   48%
4. Distribution of customer data to agents   41%
5. Provision of expert information   38%
6. Integration of partner into business processes   31%
7. Training of sales people   18%
8. Payment of premium   3%
9. Contract information   3%
10. Integration of customer   3%

In this context it is interesting that integration of partners in existing processes was only rated by 31% as important. Training of sales people was regarded as not important.

Looking at these processes it can be clearly stated that processes no. 1 and no. 3 shall be speeded up as well as cut in cost by providing them over the net. However, no. 2 in the authors opinion has to be regarded slightly differently. Of course, there is a speed and cost aspect connected with it since double work is avoided by it. It can also be seen as a step towards improving customer service since the intermediary has first hand information due to its integration into the business processes. That way a company is able to demonstrate customer orientation by lean processes, short ways of decision-making and little administration – and thus create advantage over its competitors.

In the interviews, the CIO's stated that in principle each business process with partners and customers can be handled digitally, since it is in most cases information interchange, i.e. exchange of documents via e-mail or data file transfer. One CIO was of the opinion that the investigation record in a loss investigation case has to be on paper since a digital signature is not accepted as yet and these are very important documents.

In more detail, the executives were of the opinion that, for example, all information interchange processes between administration offices –especially with car license offices that are largely handled by EDI today - or banks could be done via the web at much lower cost. In addition the whole process of information interchange related to statistics in association with German insurance companies could be handled in this way. To sum up there is a lot of potential to perform processes via the web cheaper and faster that are currently handled by interchange of cassettes or EDI.

In this connection it is very interesting that, of those groups with whom information management was rated very important (5) partners were highest at 19% and of those groups information management was rated important (4) customers were the highest at 43%.

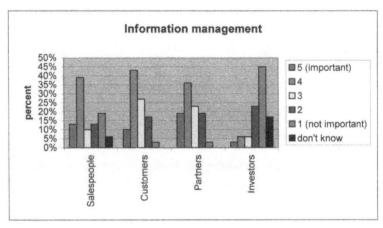

FIGURE 40: INFORMATION MANAGEMENT

Taking together these groups rated at 4 and 5 there is almost the same focus and importance rated for partners, customers and salespeople. Investors are playing a minor role. An explanation for this could be that a lot of insurance companies are still institutions under public law.

Area	%
Partners	55
Customers	53
Sales people	52
Investors	9

To sum up it can be argued that there are large similarities between the Business-to-Business and the Business-to-Customer areas concerning information management.

6.7 Focused areas

In order to get insight into which strategic direction German insurance companies are
following concerning electronic commerce and with it competitive advantage, an open
question on the areas the several companies are focusing upon was asked. The result
shows that most companies are tackling online services which can be counted to the pre-
sales phase and thus to the Business-to-Consumer section of electronic commerce.
However, looking at the result in some more detail and dividing the answers into the
areas of electronic commerce (B2B and B2C) the result looks as follows:

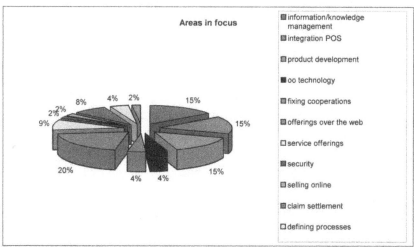

FIGURE 41: AREAS IN FOCUS

Information/knowledge management and transformation of business processes to the
POS shows that most companies have started to focus on their B2B field by
reengineering current business and information processes with intermediaries. Online
sales only amount to 2% of the respondents.

Finally, a lot of companies state that they are concentrating on product development
which confirms the statement of one CIO that current products are not suitable for
online-sales. Complex products that contain a lot of features as a package are not
suitable for online selling. Owing to the trend of personalisation new products on a
modular basis with simple insurance terms and conditions are required in order to meet
consumers' requirements.

6.8   Constraints

As far as constraints are concerned the participants of the fieldwork returned the
following result.

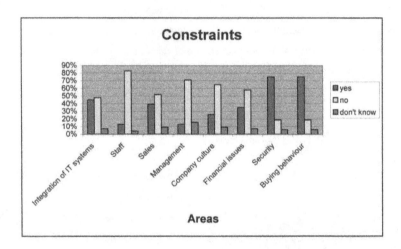

FIGURE 42: CONSTRAINTS FOR ELECTRONIC COMMERCE

The ranking of constraints is as follows:

1.	Security	75%
2.	Buying behaviour	75%
3.	Integration of current IT systems	45%
4.	Sales organisations	39%
5.	Financial issues	35%
6.	Company culture	26%
7.	Staff	13%
8.	Management	13%

Some aspects of this result are very interesting. Security together with buying behaviour
are rated number one. It is no wonder to the author that buying behaviour is ranking that
high because in these days most business is handled by intermediaries. However, it is a
bit surprising to the author that security is voted that highly. In days where homebanking
is becoming more and more popular it is not quite clear why this is rated so highly. The

interviews with CIO's revealed an opposite result. Three out of four stated that security
is definitely an important issue but no constraint. Integration of current IT systems and
existing sales organisations are rated surprisingly low for the author. A study from Booz
Allen & Hamilton stated that existing sales organisations are seen as a major constraint
for deploying electronic commerce[1]. The only explanation the author finds for this result
is that it is not anymore just a matter of selling insurance on the web but the B2B aspect
must be take account of too, by, for instance, integrating intermediaries via web to the
company's resources. With reference to the integration of current IT systems a study
from PWC revealed that technology change and integration is seen as a critical
challenge amongst 67.5% of the senior managers questioned.[2]

Company culture, staff and management are rated more or less as unimportant. This is a
clear indicator to the author that the principle of electronic commerce is not fully
understood by most participants. In the literature on the subject, these issues are the CSF
if electronic commerce is to be implemented successfully.[3] One CIO stated that existing
organisational structures are not consistent with electronic commerce. He was of the
opinion that with electronic commerce a company should not only speed up operating
and information processes but also decision making processes and that organisational
structures within his company should be pruned much flatter.

Again the author has to point to the statement of cost reduction mentioned earlier in
chapter 4.6 and that cost reduction in administration comes mainly from staff reduction.
Since it is very natural that people defend their workplaces it is doubtful whether staff
should be no constraint in implementing electronic commerce.

[1] Booz, Allen & Hamilton (1998),http://www.bah.com/press/insurance.htm
[2] Electronic Business Outlook (1999), p.12
[3] Electronic Business Outlook (1999), p. 6

6.9   Summary of fieldwork

The field work was carried out following the theoretical considerations taken from the literature in order to get evidence concerning the hypothesis that electronic commerce will provide an excellent means of creating competitive advantage for companies within the German insurance industry.

The survey revealed that senior managers think that the insurance market is going to change dramatically for the private customer segment in the forthcoming 10 years. Sales channels are expected to move into other industries such as automotive and especially online insurance via the web. Customer expectations as well as their behaviour and profiles indicates that this will very likely occur .

The main benefits of electronic commerce are seen mainly in the area of customer service followed by the reengineering of business processes. The transfer of activities from administration to the Point of Sales/ Point of Service and the provision of online ordering possibilities are of particular import in this regard.

With reference to the strategic impact of electronic commerce and the creation of competitive advantage the author found that the companies and senior managers questioned think that they could create competitive advantage by deploying Electronic commerce especially in terms of improved service quality - or say customer relationship management - as well as in online sales.

The main constraints for electronic commerce are related to security and the buying behaviour of customers.

Regarding their current actions, German insurance companies are focusing on improvement of information management either with customers in the pre-sales phase and in reengineering business processes concerning intermediaries by transferring activities to the POS.

7   Conclusions

7.1   Conclusions drawn from the literature

This dissertation has given the author a better understanding of the complex area of electronic commerce and its different possibilities. Through the reading of literature, articles and studies, the author has been able to broaden his knowledge on the subject of electronic commerce and the areas affected by it.

On the basis of a literature review and examples taken from other industries, the author has come to the conclusion that electronic commerce has not only the potential to change the industry structure, business processes and CSF of the German insurance industry but also the whole economy. Industry boundaries will amalgamate and the rules of competition will change.

The old model of Porter's generic strategies is not sufficient anymore in order to determine the sources of competitive advantage in cost-leadership and differentiation. Speed (time-to-market) and especially flexibility are two factors that companies have to take into consideration as well. With the internet and its cost-cutting effect on transactions and information interchange in combination with the deployment of modern software applications, the focus on cost leadership has to be questioned especially in mature markets where products develop into commodities. This development can best be observed in the car insurance market where a price war has been taking place since the deregulation of the German insurance market. Even if the German insurance industry has a lot of catching up to do in terms of efficiency owing to its long regulation until 1994 they will only be able to create competitive advantage in the long run by offering unique and personalised products and services. Through the direct interaction with customers and the possibility of one-to-one marketing by establishing customer profiles and preferences electronic commerce enables a company to establish long term customer relations.

This in turn requires sophisticated software applications that enable the companies to establish virtual value chains and the creation of customer profiles.

As a whole the author has come to the conclusion that electronic commerce is imperative for insurance companies if they want to create competitive advantage - or to put it in another way – survive in the future.

7.2 Conclusions drawn from the fieldwork

The fieldwork has given the author a better understanding of the specific characteristics, problems and opinions of electronic commerce within the German insurance industry. Furthermore, the author has gained a deeper insight into the current thinking of senior management within the German insurance industry.

On the basis of the fieldwork undertaken, by questionnaire and some interviews with CIO's, the author has come to the conclusion that the persons questioned have identified the web as a suitable medium for the distribution of insurance and servicing of customers.

With reference to the creation of competitive advantage it can be stated that electronic commerce is seen as a suitable means of doing so. However, owing to the areas the companies under review are currently focusing upon, the author has come to the conclusion that German insurance companies have just started work on the subject of electronic commerce and in comparison to other industries such as financial services have a lot of catching up to do.

However, the author has got the impression from the questioned persons and interview partners that most of these insurance companies have not fully understood the requirements connected with EC:creating virtual value chains in order to add value to the physical value chains in combination with a consequent customer orientation (one-to-one marketing; mass customisation).

The main constraints for implementing Electronic commerce are seen in security, buying behaviour of customers and integration of current legacy systems.

7.3   Final conclusions-correlations between the literature and fieldwork

Based on a review of the literature and the fieldwork undertaken, the author has come to the following final conclusions.

Both the literature and the fieldwork reveal that electronic commerce will have a significant impact on the insurance industry and is going to cause major changes in sales channels as well as in business processes. However, the destruction of current value chains owing to a reduction in transaction costs and the needed concentration on core competences in order to create value in an increasingly competitive environment has not been identified by German insurance companies so far. Concentration on one of the three core processes (CRM, product development, infrastructure) as outlined earlier is, in the authors opinion, the logical consequence for a mature and highly competitive environment.

Without any doubt there is agreement between theory and practice on the suitability of products and services for electronic commerce. The same can be stated for the areas and sources for creating competitive advantage. In particular, these are improved customer service (CRM) and reengineering of business processes within the business-to-business field, mostly the integration of business partners – especially intermediaries (agents/brokers) by streamlining business processes by transferring activities to the point of sales or point of service.

With reference to the areas focused upon and the relatively high response for product development, there are signs that online insurance will increase in the near future. The trend of mature markets – shifting from mass markets towards mass customisation – is a driver for EC in general and will have its impact on the insurance industry as well.

However, the fieldwork gave the author the impression that the future winners will not come from existing insurance companies but from new foundations that start with new visions, products, services and sales channels since they do not have any burdens of the past.

8   Recommendations

electronic commerce is going to change the rules of doing business within the insurance industry. Besides a greater focus on cost-efficiency, differentiation, i.e.customisation and personalisation of products and services, will become imperative in order to create competitive advantage in a global networked economy.

On the basis of the findings of this dissertation the author has developed a framework for the successful implementation of electronic commerce principles.

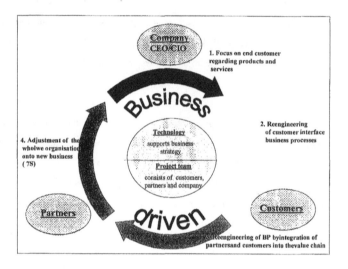

FIGURE 43: FRAMEWORK OF IMPLEMENTATION OF EC PRINCIPLES

1. Insurers have to reengineer their business processes along the whole value chain in order to be prepared for the new way of competing. This does not only concern the processes between business partners and customers but also inhouse processes. Electronic commerce does not end on a company's web server. Companies who ignore this fact will be the future losers. This implies that companies have to adjust themselves strategically to fit the new rules. Companies who have successfully integrated electronic commerce have integrated their customers and business partners into their business processes.

2. When companies start implementing EC they should always bear in mind that electronic commerce is business- (or market-) and not technology-driven. Technology is just the means that is supporting business. Of course technology does play an important role, especially when different legacy systems have to be integrated, but the focus of all activities should always be the customer and his expectations and preferences. Therefore the author recommends that project teams should not consist of too many IT-people.

3. Furthermore, companies should remember that new business rules and new business processes always imply change. In order to manage this change successfully, senior management must provide their commitment and support. Senior management (CIO, CEO) and the project team itself are the keys to successful implementation of any EC-strategy. Clearly, successful implementation of an EC-strategy normally requires a holistic approach, i.e. EC has to be a part of the company's business strategy that normally requires the adjustment of the whole company (systems, style, staff, skills, shared values, structure and strategy).

4. As mentioned above, new rules require change and change has to be managed. This aspect should not be taken too lightlyas it is probably the most challenging part of introducing electronic commerce. This has been proven in many companies that have changed their strategic approach. This does not only include new organizational structures (flatter hierarchies, shorter ways of decision making) but also a new culture or spirit within a company.

5. With reference to the German insurance industry the author recommends that companies should not orient themselves on existing business processes and rules but should inform themselves about best practice stories from other industries.

6. The implementation of electronic commerce does not only require integration of systems, partners and customers but also systems that allow the gathering, organising, selecting and synthesising of information. Datawarehousing, data-mining and customer profiles are the key words that have to be mentioned when a company is talking about electronic commerce.

9   Appendices

9.1   Appendix 1:

Premium income

Insurance lines	1998 +/- in %	1998 TPI*	1997 +/- in %	1997 TPI*	1996 +/- in %	1996 TPI*	1995 +/- in %	1995 TPI*	1994 TPI*
Life	4.4	102.60	5.80	98.30	5.00	92.80	6.50	88.40	82.90
Health	6.1	38.0	4.40	35.80	7.20	34.40	13.50	32.10	28.30
P & C	-2.2	92.9	-0.90	95.00	0.00	96.00	3.10	96.00	93.20
Total	1.9	233.50	2.50	229.10	3.00	223.20	5.90	216.50	204.40
Social insurance	-	-	5.00	709.00	5.00	675.50	-	643.20	-

*Total premium income in bill. DM

9.2   Appendix 2:

Growth of internet population:

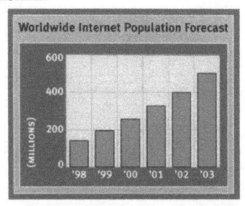

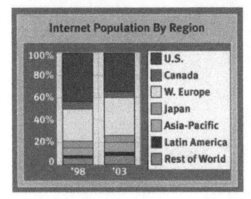

Internet Population Forecast Detail				
	1998		2003	
	USERS*	%	USERS*	%
U.S.	62.8	44%	177.0	35%
Canada	8.8	6%	23.6	5%
W. Europe	40.9	29%	168.4	34%
Japan	8.0	6%	32.0	6%
Asia-Pacific	10.2	7%	47.7	9%
Latin America	3.0	2%	14.8	3%
Rest of World	8.5	6%	38.9	8%
Total	142.2	100%	502.4	100%

* IN MILLIONS. SOURCE: INTERNATIONAL DATA CORP.

9.3   *Appendix 3: Questionnaire*

Survey on insurances and e-commerce

Part I: general questions obout your company

1   About yourself:

a) Your function (please specify): ....

b) Are you:
  ☐ IT-department   ☐ Senior management
  ☐ Sales   ☐ Administration

2   About your company

What kind of insurance/ financial services are you offering?

☐   P&C   ☐   Health insurance

☐   Car insurance   ☐   Investments products

☐   Life insurance   ☐   Legal expenses

3   What is the total premium income of your company?

☐	☐	☐
< 750 Mio	750 Mio>1,5 Mrd	> 1,5 Mrd.

What percentage is car insurance?

4   What sales channels are you operating?

☐	☐	☐	☐	☐
direct agents	broker	direct	internet	banks

☐	☐	
car dealer	other	
	please specify	

Part II: Questions on e-commerce / internet

II	5	Do you think the internet is a suitable sales channel for insurances?	□ yes	□ no	□ don't know		

6. If yes, what kinds of insurance do you think are suitable to be sold over the internet?
(multiple responses accepted)

	yes	no	don't know
Car insurances	□	□	□
Travel health insurance	□	□	□
Life- / annuity insurance	□	□	□
Health insurance	□	□	□
Accident insurance	□	□	□
Legal expenses insurance	□	□	□
Property insurances (building, household9	□	□	□
Private liability insurance	□	□	□
Investment products	□	□	□

Other, please specify _____

7. If not, why do you think the internet is not an appropriate sales channel?
(multiple responses accepted)

□ Complexity of product	□ Buying behaviour
□ Security risks	□ Legal constraints
□ Regulatory restrictions	□ Other, please specify

_____

8	Do you think the internet is a suitable medium to service customers?	□ yes	□ no	□ don't know

9. If yes, which of the following features do you or will you offer to your customrers in which time frame?

	Already offered	1-2 years	3-4 years	>4 years	Not at all
- make administrative changes	□	□	□	□	□
- announcement of claims	□	□	□	□	□
- track status of claims	□	□	□	□	□

- Adjust coverage	☐	☐	☐	☐	☐
- consultancy tools for analysing insurance needs	☐	☐	☐	☐	☐
- Product information	☐	☐	☐	☐	☐
- Ratios from insurance companies, such as premium income, profit etc.	☐	☐	☐	☐	☐
- Price examples for diverse kinds of insurance	☐	☐	☐	☐	☐
- Possibility to calculating personal price examples	☐	☐	☐	☐	☐
- Ordering of personal offers	☐	☐	☐	☐	☐
- Online fixing of appointments	☐	☐	☐	☐	☐
- Self help book on insurance issues/ questions	☐	☐	☐	☐	☐
- Job offerings	☐	☐	☐	☐	☐
- Non-insurance related offerings such as link-lists, games,	☐	☐	☐	☐	☐
- Discussion groups on insurance issues	☐	☐	☐	☐	☐

10   How would you rate the impact and benefits of e-commerce on the strategic adjustment of your organization?

	Important 5				Not important 1	Don't know
- Hive off business pro-cesses, focus on core competences	☐	☐	☐	☐	☐	☐
- Fix new cooperations	☐	☐	☐	☐	☐	☐
- Focus on target groups	☐	☐	☐	☐	☐	☐
- Change sales channels, e.g brokers,	☐	☐	☐	☐	☐	☐
- Offer a wider range of products and services	☐	☐	☐	☐	☐	☐
- Specialisation on products	☐	☐	☐	☐	☐	☐
- Development of new products	☐	☐	☐	☐	☐	☐
- Enter new markets	☐	☐	☐	☐	☐	☐

11 How would you rate the impact and usefulness of e-commerce on information management of your organization?

	Important 5				Not important 1	Don't know
- Providing salespeople with relevant information	☐	☐	☐	☐	☐	☐
- Providing customers with relevant information	☐	☐	☐	☐	☐	☐
- Providing partners with relevant information	☐	☐	☐	☐	☐	☐
- Providing investors with relevant information	☐	☐	☐	☐	☐	☐
- Education/training of sales staff	☐	☐	☐	☐	☐	☐

12 What do you think about the usefulness of e-commerce on the following business processes ?

	Good 5				Bad 1	Don't know
- Handle claim settlement	☐	☐	☐	☐	☐	☐
- Transfer activities to the point of sale , e.g policy issuing	☐	☐	☐	☐	☐	■
- Software distribution for calculation programmes	☐	☐	☐	☐	☐	■
- Transformation of customer data to the salespeople	☐	☐	☐	☐	☐	■
- Download of forms for salesforce	☐	☐	☐	☐	☐	■
- Make information available for experts	☐	☐	☐	☐	☐	☐
- Linking business partners with your organization, e.g. hospitals, repair centres, experts	☐	☐	☐	☐	☐	■

13 Do you think that e-commerce will reduce your operating-costs?

☐	☐	☐
yes	no	don't know

If yes in which areas ?
(multiple reponses possible)

☐	☐	☐	☐	■
Sales	Marketing	Administration	Product development	Se

14 If yes, how big would you estimate your savings in 5 years time? _____%

16 Do you think that e-commerce will increase you revenue?

☐	☐	☐
yes	no	don't know

17 If yes, how big would you estimate your increase in 5 years time? _____%

18 Where do you see the main benefits in e-commerce?

☐	☐	☐	☐
cost savings	revenue increase	enhance service/ quality	time-to – market

19 Do you think that you will reach competitive advantage through EC?

☐	☐	☐
yes	no	don't know

20   If yes, in which areas?

21   Which of the following points could be an obstacle in implementing an e-commerce strategy?

(multipe responses accepted)

	yes	no	don't know
Integration of current IT-systems	☐	☐	☐
Inhouse staff	☐	☐	☐
Sales organization	☐	☐	☐
Management	☐	☐	☐
Company culture	☐	☐	☐
Financial resources	☐	☐	☐
Security	☐	☐	☐
Human resources	☐	☐	☐

Other, please specify:

22   How would you rate the impact of e-commerce on the

	1 low	2	3	4	5 high
a) organizational structure of your company?	☐	☐	☐	☐	☐
b) on the inhouse business processes?	☐	☐	☐	☐	☐
c) IT-systems	☐	☐	☐	☐	☐
d) Sales channels	☐	☐	☐	☐	☐

23   Has your company already started to integrate e-commerce into your corporate strategy?

    ☐ yes   ☐ no   ☐ don't know

24   If yes, please name the 3 main issues you are focusing upon.

25   What do you think are the key success factors in implementing these e-commerce features ?

Thank you for your cooperation!!

9.4   Appendix 4: Interview guide

Interview guide E-Commerce:

1. Industry structure:

What are the macro-environment impacts? What are the new PEST according to the networked economy?

Political

Economic

Social

Technological

How will the 5-forces develop in a networked economy?

Customers

Suppliers

Substitutes

New entrants

Existing competitors

What are the new market rules? Is speed everything? Price? Personalization?

How will the internet change current systems and rules?

What are the critical success factors for insurance companies for the future?

2. Products and services

What products are suitable to be sold over the internet?

Will products change? How? What do customers expect?

What kind of services are suitable for the internet? Will they change?

What new services will be needed with EC?

3. Strategic impact of internet/EC?

What is the benefit of EC for the strategic alignment ?

Which strategies does EC support best?

What will be the strategic options an insurance company is faced with in future?

What are the best EC strategies for insurance companies?

4. Value chain

How will the value chain be affected by EC and the internet?

Modern management literature talks about focusing on core competences especially on three core processes if a company wants to create competitive advantage on the long run in a networked economy .

  a) Focus on Customer –Relation Management

  b) Focus on product development

  c) Focus on infrastructure

Where do you see the core competences of insurance companies in the future?

What role do intermediaries play in the future?

Do you think that there are new intermediaries emerging?

5. Competitive advantage

How can insurance companies create competitive advantage through EC?

Cost, time, distribution, improvement in customer service, improvement of competitive situation?

Do you think you will increase your revenues and premium income? How much in what time frame?

Do you think you can cut cost? How much in what time frame? In which areas?(see questionnaire)

6. Business processes

What kind of business processes in the B2C field can be depicted by EC?

When are you planning selling online?

What kind of BP are suitable for the B2B field? (garages, hospitals, reinsurance, intermediaries etc.)

How can virtual value chains be created?

7. Organizational implications

What are the organizational implications of EC?

Structure, leadership, change management, processes, staff (headcount), sales organizations, company culture

Where are the main constraints for EC?

Legal aspects

Security

Technology integration

Sales organizations

What areas are you concentrating on (tackled already)?

What are the CSF in implementing an EC strategy?

9.5   *Appendix 5:*

Where do you see as the main advantages in online shopping?

feature	total %
sufficient informations on products/services	39,9%
range of products/services	43,6%
price comparisons	52,5%
uncomplicated ordering	56,6%
time-saving shopping	62,3%
independence from shopping hours	81,9%
convienience	66,8%
no advantages	8,0%

10 Bibliography

Albers Sönke / Clement Michel / Peters Kay / Skiera Bernd; eCommerce- Einstieg, Strategie und Umsetzung im Unternehmen, Frankfurt am Main 1999

Andersen Consulting (1999),What's the value of e-commerce, http://www.ac.com(showcase/ecommerce/ecom_whats_the_value.html (4.9.1999)

Baumann Martina / Kistner Andreas C., e-Business, Vaterstetten 1999

Bechmann Torsten; Entwicklungsperspektiven des Electronic Commerce in der Versicherungswirtschaft; in Versicherungswirtschaft, Volume 53, p 1254- 1258, Karlsruhe 1998

Berryman Kenneth, Harrington Lorraine, Layton-Rodin Dennis, Rerolle Vincent, Three emerging strategies, The McKinsey Quarterly 1998, No. 1 pp.152-159

Bliemel Friedhelm/ Fassott Georg/ Theobald Axel; Electronic Commerce, Wiesbaden 1999

Brinkmann Theodor, Die demographische Entwicklung in Deutschland und ihre Kon-sequenzen für die Versicherungswirtschaft, Karlsruhe; Verlag Versicherungswirtschaft 1991

Booz, Allen & Hamilton, Insurance study, http://www.bah.com/press/insurance.htm, (12.4.99)

Cameron Boby/Deutsch Waverly/Walker Michele/Hermsdorf Leslie; Driving IT's Externalization, 1999 http://www.forrester.com

Clement Michel, Peters Kay, Preiß Friedrich J., Electronic Commerce, in Marketing mit interaktiven Medien, Frankfurt am Main, 1998

Datamonitor; Direktversicherung in Deutschland: Der Weg zur Profitabilität, (1998)

Electronic BusinessOutlook, PricewaterhouseCoopers,
http://www.pwcglobal.com/extweb/ncsurvres.nsf/docid/D290CD558B9A6283852566B
70073218B?OpenDocument, (1999)

E-Business Technology Forecast, PricewaterhouseCoopers, Menlo Park 1999

Evans Philip B./ Wurster Thomas S. , Stragegy and the new Economics of Information,
in Creating Value in the Network Economy, Boston 1999

Feilmeier Manfred, Internet macht Umbau der Strukturen zwingend, in
Computerwoche, Heft Nr. 50, 1998 p. 59-60

Fink Dietmar H., Mass Customization, in Marketing mit interaktiven Medien, Frankfurt
am Main 1998

Fittkau Susanne/ Maaß Holger; WWW-Benutzer-Analyse- W3B-Uni-Ergebnisband,
Hamburg 1999

Forrester Research, The future of online sales,

Gabor Andreas, Internetstrategien für Versicherungsunternehmen,
Versicherungswirtschaft, Volume 54, No. 8 1999, pp. 516-519

GfK-Aktiengesellschaft, http://194.175.173.244./gfk/presse.php3? (8.6.99)

Grant Robert M., Contemporary Strategy Analysis, Oxford (1995)

Garven, James R. / Wright William H., Electronic Commerce in the Insurance Industry:
Business Perspectives, Atlanta 1998; http://www.rmictr.gsu.edu/ctr

Hagel John / Singer Marc; Das Unternehmen entflechten und klar fokussieren; Harvard
Business Manager, Volume 21, No. 5 1999, pp 61-70

Hermanns Arnold / Sauter Michael, Management Handbuch Electronic Commerce, München 1999

Hess Oliver, Internet, Electronic Data Interchange (EDI) und SAP R/3- Synergien und Abgrenzungen im Rahmen des Electronic Commerce, in Management Handbuch Electronic Commerce, München 1999

Hünerberg Reinhard/ Mann Andreas; Online-Service , in Electronic Commerce, Wiesbaden 1999

INEAS Insurance Company, http://www.ineas.com

Kasten Hans-H. Dr., Service- und Effizienzsteigerung durch Einsatz moderner Technik im Versicherungsaußendienst; Versicherungswirtschaft, Volume 52, No. 15 1997, pp1091-1094

Klein Stefan/ Selz Dorian; The Impact of Electronic Commerce on the Automotive Industry,

Koch Gottfried / Wagner Fred, Electronic Commerce in der Versicherungswirtschaft, Versicherungswirtschaft, Volume 53, No. 23 1998, p. 1643-1649

Köhler Thomas, Aufbau eines digitalen Vertriebs, Electronic Commerce, München 1997

Körner Jochen, Zukünftige Strategien in der Versicherungswirtschaft,in e-business, Frankfurt 1999

Kotler Philip, Marketing Management, New Jersey 1994

Kühlmann Knut, Prof. Dr./ Kurtenbach W./ Käßler-Pawelka Günter, Prof. Dr.; Versicherungsmarketing, Frankfurt a.M., 1995

Kurz Eberhard/ Ortwein Eckhard, Integrierte Unternehmensstrategien für Electronic Commerce im Business-to-Business Bereich – Bedeutung, Konzeption und Fallbeispiele von Business Networks, in Management Handbuch Electronic Commerce, München 1999

Lier Monika, Dies und das aus der elektronischen Versicherungswelt, Versicherungswirtschaft, Volume 54, No. 20 1999; pp. 1484-1489

Margheiro Lynn, Henry Dave, Cooke Sandra, Montes Sabrina, The Emerging Digital Economy, Washington 1998, http://www.ecommerce.gov

Magnus, Stephan; Intracommerce - das digitale Marktprinzip : Unternehmenskommunikation im Zeitalter des Internet - Remseck 1997.

Mummert & Partner, http://www.mummert.de/deutsch/press/ppbz0209.html

Mummert & Partner, http://www.mummert.de/deutsch/press/990509.html

Muth Michael, Mit Sicherheit gewinnen: Spitzenleistungen sind nötig; Karlsruhe 1982

Muth Michael, Versicherungswirtschaft, Volume 49, No. 5 1994, pp 288-298

Muther Andreas, Electronic Customer Care- Die Anbieter Kunden-Beziehung im Informationszeitalter, Berlin Heidelberg 1999

OECD: The Economic and Social Impacts of Electronic Commerce: Preliminary Findings and Resarch Agenda (1998), http://www. oecd.org/subject/e_commerce/

Peppers Don, Rogers Martha, The One-to-One Future, London 1994

Peters Thomas J./ Waterman Robert H., Auf der Suche nach Spitzenleistungen- Was man von den bestgeführtesten US-Unternehmen lernen kann; Landsberg am Lech 1986

Porter Michael E., Competitive Advantage- Creataing and Sustaining Superior Performance, New York 1985

Price Waterhouse Coopers, E-Business Technology Forecast, Menlo Park 1999

Price Waterhouse Coopers, E-Business Outlook, 1999

Rohrbach Peter, Electronic Commerce im Business-to-Business Bereich, in Management Handbuch Electronic Commerce, München 1999

Priess Stefan, Heinemann Christopher, Erfolgsfactoren des electronic Commerce, in Management Handbuch Electronic Commerce, München 1999

Rost Harald R. / Schulz-Wolfgramm Cornelius; e-business-Die Schlacht zwischen Innovation und Tradition, Frankfurt am Main 1999

Rayport Jeffrey F. / Sviokla John J. ; Exploiting the Virtual Value Chain, in Creating Value in the Network Economy, Boston 1999

Remenyi Dan/ Williams Brian/ Money Arthur/Swartz Ethne'; Doing Research in Business and Management- An Introduction to Process and Method, London 1998

Schinzer Heiko, Auswahl einer geeigneten Electronic Commerce-Strategie, in Electronic Commerce, München 1997

Scheit Alexander Dr./ Internet, neue Chancen für die Automobilindustrie, in e-business, Frankfurt 1999

Schreiber Gerhard Andreas, Electronic Commerce- Business in digitalen Medien, Neuwied 1998

See Dianne, Germany will lead European E-commerce Market, study says, See Dianne, http://www.thestandard.net/articles/article_display/0,1449,1256,00.html (29.7.99)

Schwarz Gunther, Freese Christopher, Christopher Jacques, Vergessen Sie E-Commerce, in Versicherungswirtschaft, Volume 54, No. 20 1999, pp. 1498-1504

Seybold Patricia B., Customers.com, New York 1998

Siebel Thomas M. / House Pat; Cyber Rules- Strategies for excelling at e-business; New York 1999

Siebel Thomas M. / Malone Michael; Virtual selling- going beyond the automated sales force to achieve total sales quality, New York 1996

Statistical Yearbook of German Insurance 1998, Karlsruhe 1998

Strauß Ralf E./ Schoder Detlev, Electronic Commerce-Herausforderungen aus Sicht der Unternehmen, in Management Handbuch Electronic Commerce, München 1999

Szyperski Norbert/ Klein Stefan, Referenzmodell zum Electronic Commerce, www.uni-koeln.de/wiso-fak/veroeffentlichungen/e-commerce.htm (28.11.99)

Thome Rainer Dr./ Schinzer Heiko Dr, Electronic Commerce, München 1997

Ulhaas Wolfgang, Scharek Bernhard, Die Bedeutung des Internets für die Assekuranz, Bayrischer Monatsspiegel, 1999

Weiber Rolf / Jacob F.; Kundenbezogene Informationsgewinnung, in Technischer Vertrieb- Grundlagen , Berlin 1995

Weiber Rolf / Kollmann Tobias, Wertschöpfungsprozesse und Wettbewerbsvorteile im Marketspace, in Electronic Commerce, Wiesbaden 1999

Wetzel Robert O., Paradigmenwechsel im Vertrieb, Versicherungswirtschaft, Volume 53, No. 4 1998, pp 258-259

Diplomarbeiten Agentur

Die Diplomarbeiten Agentur vermarktet seit 1996 erfolgreich
Wirtschaftsstudien, Diplomarbeiten, Magisterarbeiten, Dissertationen
und andere Studienabschlußarbeiten aller Fachbereiche und Hochschulen.

Seriosität, Professionalität und Exklusivität prägen unsere Leistungen:

- Kostenlose Aufnahme der Arbeiten in unser Lieferprogramm
- Faire Beteiligung an den Verkaufserlösen
- Autorinnen und Autoren können den Verkaufspreis selber festlegen
- Effizientes Marketing über viele Distributionskanäle
- Präsenz im Internet unter **http://www.diplom.de**
- Umfangreiches Angebot von mehreren tausend Arbeiten
- Großer Bekanntheitsgrad durch Fernsehen, Hörfunk und Printmedien

Setzen Sie sich mit uns in Verbindung:

Diplomarbeiten Agentur
Dipl. Kfm. Dipl. Hdl. Björn Bedey –
Dipl. Wi.-Ing. Martin Haschke ––––
und Guido Meyer GbR ––––––––

Hermannstal 119 k ––––––––––
22119 Hamburg ––––––––––

Fon: 040 / 655 99 20 ––––––––
Fax: 040 / 655 99 222 ––––––––

agentur@diplom.de ––––––––
www.diplom.de ––––––––

www.ingramcontent.com/pod-product-compliance
Lightning Source LLC
La Vergne TN
LVHW092340060326
832902LV00008B/745